THE BEGINNER'S GUIDE TO COLOUR PSYCHOLOGY

ANGELA WRIGHT

Angela Wright became interested in colour when she was assisting in the management of her family's hotel in the English Lake District. She subsequently made a formal study of psychology in London and of colour in California. She has been practising as a colour psychologist in the commercial marketplace for over ten years, advising clients as diverse as HM Prisons, Shell International and Mothercare on colour choice for institutions, retail space and packaging. Numerous newspapers and magazines have featured her work, and two British universities have begun research into her theories of colour harmony and colour psychology. She lives in London.

'As a marketing man, I have worked with colour for twenty-five years. This lady knows more about it than anyone I have met in that time. GRAHAM WHITE, CHAIRMAN, LONDIS GROUP

'What is important about Angela is that she has a "good eye for colour", and that, like any scientist, she likes continually to ask, "Why?" When she see colours that work well together, she asks why their particular combination is successful, she asks why the multitudes of blues are all different to one another in their effects, and she asks why the same colour works well in one environment, such as a supermarket, but not in another, such as a maximum security prison.' FROM THE FOREWORD BY CHRIS MCMANUS, PROFESSOR OF PSYCHOLOGY, UNIVERSITY COLLEGE, LONDON

'Angela Wright goes unerringly to the heart of any question of colour. At the first attempt, she provided a colour scheme for shops that succeeded – and she could explain why it worked. CHRISTOPHER BELL, MANAGING DIRECTOR, LADBROKE RACING LTD

'I was Mr Sceptical of Trowbridge. But, five years on, the designs Angela Wright helped to produce are still as fresh as ever. She suggested colours I would never have thought of. It was very successful from our point of view, and this was reflected in our sales figures.' CHARLES DAWSON, MANAGING DIRECTOR, BOWYERS (WILTSHIRE) LTD

Angela Wright conducts seminars, courses and workshops in colour psychology. For further information, contact her at Colour Affects on 0171 976 6359.

THE BEGINNER'S GUIDE TO COLOUR PSYCHOLOGY

ANGELA WRIGHT

with a foreword by Chris McManus,
MA, MD, PhD, Professor of Psychology,
University College, London

Kyle Cathie Limited

Beauty is truth, truth beauty – that is all
ye know on earth, and all ye need to know
Ode on a Grecian Urn
John Keats *1795–1821*

This book is dedicated to Baba, with love

First published in Great Britain in 1995 by
Kyle Cathie Limited
20 Vauxhall Bridge Road London SW1V 2SA

Reprinted 1998

ISBN 1 85626 286 3

Original photography on pages 61, 63, 65, 67, 69 © 1995 Nic Barlow
See also further copyright acknowledgements on page 6

Angela Wright is hereby identified as the author of this work in accordance
with Section 77 of the Copyright, Designs and Patents Act 1988.

A Cataloguing in Publication record for this title is available from the
British Library.

Edited by Caroline Taggart
Printed in Singapore

CONTENTS

ACKNOWLEDGEMENTS

Many wonderful people have contributed to my understanding of colour, and supported the idea of this book, over the years; I send them my warmest thanks.

Very special acknowledgement must go, however, to the following, whose love, support and interest were quite exceptional:

Lorea

Victoria

Richard and Angela Martin

John

Percy...

...and finally, the saintly Caroline Taggart, who managed to combine gentle sensitivity and humour with firm insistence on proper syntax in editing *The Beginner's Guide to Colour Psychology.*

Picture Credits

Nic Barlow: pages 46, 61 (all), 63 (all), 65 (top), 67 (all), 69 (both)

Photographers' Library: front cover, back cover bottom right, pages 27, 59, 98, 134 (bottom); Vax Ltd: back cover top left, page 142; Elizabeth Whiting & Associates: back cover top right (Pam Elson), pages 51 (both, top Andreas V. Einsiedel), 92 (Michael Dunne/Katrin Tolleson), 95 (Michael Dunne/Katrin Tolleson), 103 (top Tom Leighton/Hoyer-Miller, centre Tom Leighton), 106 (top Tom Leighton, bottom Frank Herholdt), 107 (Brian Harrison), 110 (top Gary Chowetz, bottom Pam Elson); Heather Angel: back cover bottom left, page 32; Science Photo Library: frontispiece (Martin Dohrn), page 10 (Keith Kent); John Watts: pages 26, 33 (both), 80, 82, 86; Planet Earth Pictures: page 34 (top, Hans Christian Heap); John Glover Photography: page 34 (bottom); Christie's Images: page 52 (left); Elizabeth Gage Ltd: page 52 (right); Gary Italiaander: page 65 (bottom); Andrea V. Einsiedel/Homes & Gardens/Robert Harding Syndication: page 88; Arcaid: page 94 (Justin Paul), 103 (bottom, Lucinda Lambton), 127 (Richard Bryant), 134 (top, Chris Gascoigne); Art Directors: pages 114, 131 (both), 138; Barclays Bank plc: page 139; Rolls-Royce Motor Cars Ltd: page 146; Porsche Cars Great Britain Ltd: page 147 (top); Sara-Jane Vere Nicoll: p. 147 (bottom) Cadbury Ltd: page 150; Bowyers (Wiltshire) Ltd: page 159 (top); Walls/Kerry Foods: page 159 (bottom); Fitch Design Consultants Ltd: page 166, 182; Ladbroke Racing Ltd: page 174 (both); RSCG Conran Design Ltd: page 178, 179; The Londis Group: page 183.

The artwork on pages 14, 22, 39, 41, 43 and 45 is by Richard Sibley.

Cover design by Andrea Purdie.

FOREWORD

by Chris McManus, MA, MD, PhD,
Professor of Psychology, University College, London

A world without colour is not just a drab and dreary world, it is also a dangerous, unpredictable world in which it is easy to be poisoned. Colour, as Angela Wright emphasizes in this book, is in some way telling us about the chemical compositions of objects – if you like, a form of psychological spectroscopy. That colour alone is the principal cue to composition is easily seen by changing the colour of objects and observing our response to them. The Colour Museum, based in Bradford, had an advertising leaflet which showed simply a plate of attractive-looking food in one half, and in the other half a monochrome version of the same plate. Now the peas were grey, the broccoli almost black, and the off-white potatoes marked with grey patches. If we were presented with that wrongly coloured food, although rationally we would all know it was the same food, more than likely it would still stick in our throat. As a medical student in Birmingham, I remember boiling potatoes, dividing them into four batches, dyeing them red, orange, green and blue with food colouring and then putting them in the oven for a few minutes to toughen the outsides a little and disguise their origin. At dinner, the guests were told that the vegetables had been bought at a range of the local ethnic shops. The red and orange potatoes were much enjoyed, the green were not so popular and the blue were hardly touched.

This may seem logically irrational, but actually it makes immensely good biological sense. We have many million years of evolution helping us to spot those foods which are good to eat – the ripe, red apples – rather than those which will make us ill – the meat that is green in colour, or the potatoes with blue-black patches on the outside. Without colour, those tasks would not be possible and we would have survived less well. It is therefore hardly surprising that we have innate responses to colour, and that these are often difficult to verbalize. Nevertheless, that does not make them any less real or any less important.

What is surprising – and again Angela emphasizes the point correctly – is how little psychologists have been concerned with the effects of colour upon behaviour. Of course physicists, biochemists, physiologists and neuroscientists now have an exquisitely sophisticated theory of how we see colour, but there the theories stop. Few colour scientists seem to have any theory of what colour is really for and how it affects people beyond its mere perception. Few would be willing to go into a do-it-yourself store on a Saturday afternoon and say anything terribly sensible about the behaviour of the myriads of people all trying to find 'just the right colour' to paint the bathroom, the kitchen or the bedroom; or to explain the behaviour of shoppers looking for the right combination of blouse and skirt, or shirt and tie, so that the colours 'go together'. Most scientists simply do not see such questions as important. Just because a bathroom could, in principle, be painted any colour, it therefore does not seem sensible or worthwhile to ask why it matters which particular colour has in fact been used. But of course it does matter. It matters not because the functionality of the bathroom, as a room for removing the dirt and grime of everyday life, would be affected, but because colour tells us something important about ourselves, about the underlying way we are organized and, probably, about how we got to be this way over aeons of evolution. Colour also, of course, properly used, makes us feel better and makes the world look better, and that is no mean result either.

Angela Wright is, as she says herself 'obviously passionate about colour'. She also trained as a psychologist, although, as she candidly admits, that taught her almost nothing about colour, since there were then and still are few psychologists who consider colour psychology – or indeed questions of aesthetics and beauty in general – as important, and the topic is still hardly mentioned in degree courses. What is important about Angela is that she has 'a good eye for colour' and that, like any scientist, she likes continually to ask, 'Why?' When she sees colours that work well together she asks why their particular combination is successful, she asks why the multitude of blues are all different from one another in their effects, and she asks why the same colour works well in one environment, such as a supermarket, but not in another, such as a maximum security prison. And of course over the years she has developed her own theory as to why these things happen.

It is that theory which is presented in this book. Perhaps the central innovation of Angela's theory is that it does not emphasize the difference between colours for which we have words – red, blue, yellow, etc. – but the differences between the many forms of each of those colours – the slightly greenish blue which is a little darker and a little less saturated than the other one. This is relatively unexplored territory, in part because of the very obvious difficulty of description. It is not, however, a scientific theory. There are no experiments, no proofs, no careful testing of claims and counter-claims, no statistics, no graphs, no tables of figures. Instead there is just the encapsulated experience of someone who has spent many years pondering what colour is really about, and what are the rules that seem to work for it. As such, it is therefore the product of an artist, not a scientist, someone distilling a lifetime of personal experience. That, of course, does not mean it will not be of use to scientists.

Science in general, and psychology in particular, have changed over the past forty or fifty years. Once it was commonplace to say that if a phenomenon had no obvious scientific explanation then it must be wrong. A nice example concerns walking on a tightrope. Walking on a tightrope one foot above the ground is not that difficult, even for an amateur, but walking on one fifty feet above the ground is exceedingly difficult, as even professional tightrope walkers will explain. The clever theoretical physicist points out that the laws of balance and motion are identical in the two situations and that therefore there is no objective reason why one situation should be more difficult than the other. In fact, the explanation of the environmental psychologist is much more interesting and accepts the experience of the expert as valid. Balance depends critically on visual feedback, principally in the form of the visual flow-field, and that is less effective fifty feet above the ground. The experience of the expert transcends the simplistic view of the theoretical scientist.

Psychologists have learned, therefore, to listen to experts who have spent their lives working on specific problems, and the psychology of expertise also teaches us about the abilities and potentials of non-experts. Angela Wright is one such expert, an expert on colour. In this book she has set down, explicitly, carefully and with a wealth of example, her own formulation of how colours affect us. That is invaluable to the psychologist trying to study the effects of colour. It is also very brave, as it means that we will now be able to ask whether the rules that Angela finds are applicable to all people in all situations (and of course they may not be – that is the risk of setting oneself up for scientific investigation), and, if not, what are their limitations. If they do apply generally, then that will raise questions about process and mechanism. Scientists interested in colour will therefore thank her for her experiences. For everyone else, and that includes the scientists as well, her book will also make us think more carefully about every decision we make in our daily lives about the colours of rooms, clothes or whatever. Instead of acting without thought, we will ask why we are choosing a particular colour. And in so doing we will discover a little more of the richness of the world of colour, a world which artists have known about since the dawn of recorded history.

PART ONE

THE LANGUAGE OF COLOUR

CHAPTER ONE

The Source of Life

I f you look up the word 'colour' in a dictionary, you will find anything up to fourteen or fifteen different definitions – all of them are correct; but somehow between them they fail to capture the essence of colour. How can you explain it in mere words? It is light, the source of life; it touches and expresses the soul of mankind. There is nowhere that colour does not exist; we are constantly under its influence, whether we know it or not, and we do not need to have our eyes open to experience it. Have you ever closed your eyes and seen – even when the room is in darkness – myriad brilliant colours, many of which it would be impossible to reproduce in physical reality, dancing in front of you and around you like a kaleidoscope, or some celestial firework display?

Because the body processes colour through the eyes, we often make the mistake of imagining that it is only a matter of appearance. Colour is all about feelings, and is far, far more than a mere visual delight. It is a paradox, in that the scientific definition of colour relates entirely to light – but we see it in the dark, with our eyes closed. We dream in colour, we visualize and imagine in colour. There is an aura of colours surrounding each one of us, which most people cannot see, and are largely unaware of – but it can be captured on camera, by Kirlian photography. It is said that the colours in the aura change as our mental, emotional and physical health changes, and particularly sensitive healers can see it clearly.

Physicists explain colour in coldly scientific terms – vibrations of light, the only visible part of the electromagnetic spectrum, occupying a narrow band between microwaves and X-rays. Sir Isaac Newton demonstrated this: when he shone white light through a triangular prism, the different wavelengths refracted at different angles, showing light separated into its component parts – i.e. the spectrum, or rainbow. The story goes that he chanced upon the discovery whilst he was investigating something else entirely.

In simple terms the wavelengths consist of photons, or atmospheric particles of energy which, when they strike an object, will be absorbed or reflected, depending on the pigments that the object contains. A coloured object absorbs only the wavelengths which exactly match its own atomic structure, and reflect the rest – which is what we see. So, for example, the structure of a ripe carrot enables it to absorb all the waves except the orange ones, so we see carrots as orange.

There is another way of looking at it, illustrated in this quotation from *Mister God, This is Anna*, by Fynn:

I had explained that the yellow flower absorbed all the colours of the spectrum, with the exception of yellow, which was reflected back to the viewer. Anna had digested this bit of information for a while and then had come back with:

'Oh! Yellow is the bit it don't want!' and after a little pause, 'So its real colour is all the bits it do want.' I couldn't argue with this since I couldn't be sure what the heck a flower would want anyway.

Black is virtually total absorption and white is total reflection. It is fair to say, therefore, that the colour of something indicates its atomic structure.

My own interest in unravelling the mysteries of colour began in the family hotel where I lived as a child. My mother (and later I myself) was responsible for the ongoing interior design of fifty bedrooms, public areas – bar, restaurant, lounges etc. – behind the scenes operational work areas and offices. We had endless discussions about the best colours to use, and developed a strong instinct and considerable experience. We knew absolutely that too much yellow in a bedroom created irritable guests, whilst everyone loved predominantly pink bedrooms – but the pink had to have a contrasting colour to balance it or male guests felt uncomfortable. Red was a good idea in the bar; it encouraged conviviality – but it had to be carefully applied, or the excitement turned to aggression. Blue did not work in the restaurant. Green worked everywhere. Often these observations were not verbalized; we recognized them without debate.

Later I realized that my abiding interest in life had little to do with hotels beyond the constant opportunity they present for people-watching – I got no thrill from inventing a new culinary delight, or knowing we had the best wine list in the North of England. I left to study psychology, and discovered to my astonishment that no course available would give me any further understanding of the 'how' and 'why' behind all those fascinating insights that hotels had given me, into the way we respond to aesthetic influences and the environment in which we live, work and play. In those days, such questions were considered too esoteric for serious study, but I am not sure why it is still the case that a three-year degree course in psychology, or in design, devotes only a few days – a week at the most – to the psychology of colour.

I started my quest with a study of Freudian psychology, possibly instinctively recognizing that much of our behaviour, including our response to colour, is determined by powerful influences of which we are largely unconscious. What eventually emerged, some years later, was a clear hypothesis of how colour affects us, why different people respond to different colours and what kind of colour combinations will hold universal appeal. I have been testing and applying the theory in practical terms for over ten years and it holds true consistently.

Recently it attracted the attention of an eminent scientist, who decided – unknown to me – to put it to some preliminary tests. Using the material I

DEFINITELY DISHARMONIOUS COLOURS.

SUPPOSEDLY HARMONIOUS, BUT THERE'S
SOMETHING WRONG.

CORRECTED: WITH THE 'WRONG' GREEN REPLACED,
THE SIX COLOURS DO NOW HARMONIZE.

provided to delegates at a seminar we had both addressed, he devised a number of different ways to assess response and tested them on sixty volunteers at the university where he worked. He told me about it after he had completed the tests, and reported that they had produced remarkably high percentages of accuracy – over 80 per cent in some cases – in all but one, which had been a disappointing 27 per cent accurate. He suggested that I should come to the university and do the tests myself, under exactly the same conditions as his volunteers, and without any briefing.

It was very interesting. I went through all the tests rapidly (and accurately) until I came to one which consisted of twenty pairs of six-colour combinations, where subjects were required to state in each case whether 'a' or 'b' was the more harmonious. (My view was that it was not a matter of degree – the colour combinations either were or were not harmonious, but I knew I was being pedantic, so I said nothing.) From 1 to 8 I had no trouble in choosing, but when I looked at the alternatives for number 9, I said,

'Neither of these is harmonious.'

He said, 'I must insist that you choose one.'

I replied that I could only choose one which was marginally less disharmonious than the other, but I could not describe either of them as harmonious, so I must be allowed to qualify my choice with an asterisk. From number 10 to number 17 I had the same problem, so I had a total of nine asterisks. Numbers 18, 19 and 20 were fine. Of course, it turned out that this was the test which had produced the 27 per cent.

There were other people at this meeting, and everybody was telling me how wonderful the results were for such an early stage of research, but I was far from satisfied, and knew there was something wrong. When the meeting was over and everyone else had gone, I asked the scientist if I could have another look at the stimulus material. As we studied it together, I quickly realized that, in the nine suspect colour combinations, two greens had accidentally been transposed. He recognized that I was right, and I was delighted when he said,

'I would welcome the opportunity to subject this to the most stringent scientific study. I suspect that you have plumbed a psychological truth.'

Plumbing psychological truths had been my objective, but a bonus which I had not anticipated was the incidental discovery of physical patterns of colour. The existence of these patterns allows visual harmonizing to be done accurately by anyone, not necessarily talented – almost, as it were, by numbers.

Until now, harmonizing colour has always been considered a matter of subjective opinion, for which some people have a talent; although there are rules about it, they are rather sketchy and depend heavily on intuitive ability. It is generally accepted that some people have 'a good eye for colour' and others do not, so most people hesitate to take issue with someone else's colour choices, because they do not believe there is an objective basis for discussion. What I began to realize, as I applied my theories about patterns of colour in my work with colour psychology, was that all the shades, tones and tints in a tonal colour family which works well psychologically also have an unmistakable visual relationship which harmonizes them automatically.

Thus it becomes possible to put colours together with confidence, without necessarily having much training or experience in colour theory, secure in the knowledge that they will not clash. All that is required is to know which colours belong to which group. A point about this which is even more vital in practice is that it enables you to know what colours should *not* be put together.

This may appear to take the fun out of creating colour harmonies, but it is not so. In any other creative field, learning basic rules, virtually by rote in some cases, is perceived as the springboard from which work of pure quality can develop. A thorough technical grasp of the exact relationships between musical notes, for example, is taught in every College of Music, without fear of it stifling the creative process. A Mozart or a Leonardo, drawing his understanding and creative genius from a Higher Source, is born with the gift of seeing and translating the universal mathematical patterns underpinning the whole of life, and has no need of this basic information; for the rest of us it is reassuring to know that we can work within a technically sound framework which, whilst subjectively inspired, will work objectively.

THE BACKGROUND TO COLOUR THEORY

This book will introduce you to the two separate but inextricably linked threads of colour psychology – the four different personality types and their response to colours, and the physical properties of colours and their interaction.

The colour thinking to which I have always responded most strongly is contained in Goethe's 'Theory of Colours'. (That may initially have been because I was already familiar with this wonderful man's mind – having been surprised, at the outset of my study of Freudian psychology, to be instructed to read *Faust* Parts I and II first, before even looking at the Complete Works of Sigmund.)

Goethe was not as impressed with Sir Isaac Newton's contribution to our knowledge of colour as everyone else. Whilst he acknowledged that Newton's findings were brilliant, he disputed that they were primordial. He felt that they should be viewed in the context of Aristotle's theory, which had formed the basis of all colour work for 2000 years. Goethe saw Newton's ideas as secondary, and warned against the false notion that they replaced those of Aristotle; he urged us to see them as a progression.

Unfortunately, not many people heeded Goethe on this point, and colour work for over 200 years thereafter was built entirely around Newton's discovery of the spectrum.

Aristotle's view was that the two primary colours were white and black – light and its absence. He maintained that all colours derive from one of four elements – air, water, earth and fire. He also observed that, when we look into darkness, the first colour to appear will be blue. (Peripheral vision or night vision, governed by the rod receptors in the eye, is sensitive to blue; have you ever noticed how brightly the blue lights of an ambulance or a fire engine shine at night?) Looking towards light, where the cone receptors are functioning, the first colour we see will be yellow. Hence our perceptions of sunlight – which is pure white light – as yellow and the sky – where we are looking up into the vast blackness of space – as blue. Goethe described experiments, which anyone can do, demonstrating that this is indeed so: if you look long and hard at a solid white circle, you will begin to see it tinged, or ringed with yellow. You can often see this ring of warm colours around the moon when it is full, shining brightly, and the sky is clear. Do the same with a solid black circle and you will begin to perceive blue. Depending on the opacity of the intervening medium, other colours appear, so for instance if you look at it through water you will see all the other colours of the rainbow. Thus the true primary colours, after white and black, are blue and yellow.

The phrase 'primary colours' is potentially confusing, as it means different colours in different contexts. Pigment primaries are red, blue and yellow – mixing blue and yellow will produce green – but the primary colours when using light – in colour television, for example – are red, blue and green; yellow is a secondary light colour. These, however, are applications – Aristotle, the great philosopher, was looking beyond that level to the universal core.

Polarity is at the heart of life. We see light and dark, up and down, out and in, yang and yin, positive and negative, hot and cold, masculine and feminine. The point about polarities is that we cannot know one without the other; they are always two sides of the same coin. The great trick is finding perfect balance. Blue and yellow express polarities – cool and warm, contraction and expansion, sedation and stimulus, night and day.

In purely spectral terms, the longer wavelength colours (red, orange, yellow) relate to the sun – day, light, projection of energy, active, expansion, masculine, yang – and the shorter wavelength colours (blue, indigo, violet) relate to the moon – night, dark, containment of energy, passive, contraction, feminine, yin. Green balances both. White, which is total reflection, is yang; black is total absorption and therefore yin.

It has taken us nearly two and a half thousand years, until the end of the twentieth century, to recognize the specific link between Aristotle's ideas of four basic colour roots and other great thinkers' recognition of four personality types and their means of self expression, although a common thread, not dissimilar to this theory, linking the ideas of so many great minds over the centuries, is clearly discernible.

THE FOUR PERSONALITY TYPES

Classifications of personality types into four has remained a constant; from the Greek physician Galen's concept of four types, or 'humours', deriving from body fluids – Sanguine, Choleric, Phlegmatic and Melancholic – to twentieth-century psychology, such as Jung's four functional types, deriving from Thought, Feeling, Sensation and Intuition – agreement seems to have remained constant that we fall into four categories. No matter how individual we like to think we are (and indeed every single one of us is unique, because the permutations are virtually infinite), there are recognizable patterns of typical behaviour and characteristics which can be clearly defined. For the purpose of this book, let us define the four types in the simple categories of introvert and extrovert, light and intense, which we shall call Types I, II, III and IV.

Our recent understanding of colour also leads us to four classifications. They are built around cool, blue-based tones and warm, yellow-based tones, and within these two parameters further analysis derives from intensity. So we have four tonal families of colour – warm-toned, relatively delicate colours; cool-toned colours with the same quality of lightness and delicacy; warm-toned colours with depth and intensity; and cool-toned, strong colours. For the moment we shall describe these tonal families rather prosaically as Group I, Group II, Group III and Group IV. I will introduce you to some more poetic names later.

It is when we recognize the correlation between these patterns of colour and of human personality and response that we can begin to progress towards more precise understanding of colour psychology. The links become clear: Group I colours are warm (yellow-based) and light, Type I personalities are externally motivated and light; Group II colours are cool (blue-based) and delicate, Type II personalities are internally motivated and light. Group III colours are warm and rich, Type III personalities externally motivated and more intense. Group IV colours are cool and strong; Type IV personalities internally motivated and intense.

An important distinction should be made here; there is a difference between extrovert and externally motivated (and similarly between introvert and internally motivated). An extrovert is a person who tends to turn his personality out towards the world and express himself freely, whereas a person who is externally motivated bases his behaviour and, often, his thoughts and opinions on his perception of what others think – he is motivated from without. A person who is internally motivated could perhaps be better described as 'self-determined' – motivated from within.

The colours which appeal most to any individual are those which relate to his or her own pattern. So, for example, a Type II introvert will prefer the cool, delicate tones of Group II colours, and they will be the most supportive psychologically. (The fact that they are also the most flattering visually is a bonus.) A fiery Group III extrovert would find the cool Group II delicacy too bland and very draining, both physiologically and psychologically. Although we all have our own individuality, which makes these characteristics relative, this is the essence of each individual's make-up. I am reminded of an incident many years ago, which illustrates this: we had a young office junior – a very pretty and lively seventeen-year-old blonde, clearly Type I. As is so often the case with young people who have not yet found their own style, she virtually lived in black. One day, she arrived in the office in a vivid coral-coloured dress, and everyone commented on how good she looked. I asked her to do me a favour.

'When you get home tonight, as soon as you come through the door, would you just sit down and analyse how you feel?' I reminded her of how some days seem to be more wearing than others, for no specific reason, and she agreed. 'Tomorrow, if you go back to your usual black, could you repeat that exercise again when you get home?'

She readily undertook to do this, and on the third morning, she burst into my office. 'You're a witch!' she declared. 'How did you know? I was exhausted when I got home last night, but I could have danced all night the night before!'

I explained to her that the particular coral colour she had been wearing on the first day had actually given her more energy, whereas the introversion of black meant that she, being essentially an extrovert, had to work harder to express her personality.

In the case of mankind, the external is always a reflection of the internal, and our physical colouring does reflect, just as the colouring of a carrot reflects, our atomic structure. In the case of carrots, we recognize instinctively that we should not eat it if it is green; we know that an orange carrot is edible and indeed the colour of it creates expectations of exactly how it will taste; if a carrot is black, we throw it away. So it is with us – our colouring says it all. Avicenna, the eleventh-century Arab medical man, always took the colouring of the patient into account when making a diagnosis – he observed links between specific colouring and characteristics of personality which would predispose a patient towards particular medical conditions. It is not my intention in this book to describe in any real depth the visual patterns of physical colouring. There is already a wealth of information about that aspect of colour and, since there are blondes, brunettes, redheads and infinite variations of all three, and of all ethnic types and skin tones, in all the four personality types, it is a complex matter.

Unfortunately, however, there is also a wealth of disinformation about it, because any effort to translate definitions of the visual differences into words is virtually doomed to oversimplification and misunderstanding. Time and time again I see people who have been wrongly advised. Their personalities are struggling to get out from behind colours which are either draining them because they are too bland, straining them because they are too harsh, or extinguishing their warmth because they are cold.

We do not have adequate words to describe the precise colour variations between, for example, a cool, blue-eyed blonde and a warm, blue-eyed blonde. Using purely visual criteria is very unreliable. If we use pictures, we are at the mercy of the notoriously unreliable colour reproduction process. A much simpler and more reliable basis for analysis derives from personality traits and colour preferences. When you discover, for instance, that Margaret Thatcher is an example of a cool blonde and Diana, Princess of Wales, was a warm blonde, you begin to understand.

Understanding colour patterns, and how they combine with other physical characteristics, such as physiognomy, voice, texture of skin and hair, to manifest personality, keys us in accurately to the essential nature of a person. Knowing the properties of individual hues will tell us his or her mental state at any given moment – as expressed in the colours being worn.

CHAPTER TWO

So How Does It Work?

Before we can start to appreciate fully the wonder of colour, we need to learn the basic hues of the spectrum – 'Richard Of York Gave Battle In Vain' (Red, Orange, Yellow, Green, Blue, Indigo, Violet) – and the terminology:

HUE	'The attribute of colour which enables an observer to classify it as red, blue etc.' (Collins Dictionary)
TINT	A hue with white added
SHADE	A hue with black added
TONE	A hue with grey added
VALUE	The lightness or darkness of a colour – light colours are 'high value' and dark colours are 'low value'
CHROMA	The presence of colour
CHROMATIC INTENSITY	The percentage of colour present – also known as Saturation
MONOCHROMATIC	Containing shades, tones and tints of only one colour
ACHROMATIC	Containing no colour – i.e. black, white or pure grey
COMPLEMENTARY COLOURS	Colours opposite each other on the colour wheel

This last is a very important point when harmonizing colours, as complementary colours intensify each other. If you put red beside red, they both appear to lose some of their colour, but put green beside red and the red looks redder and the green greener. One common example of failure to understand this concept is the widespread belief that blue eye make-up

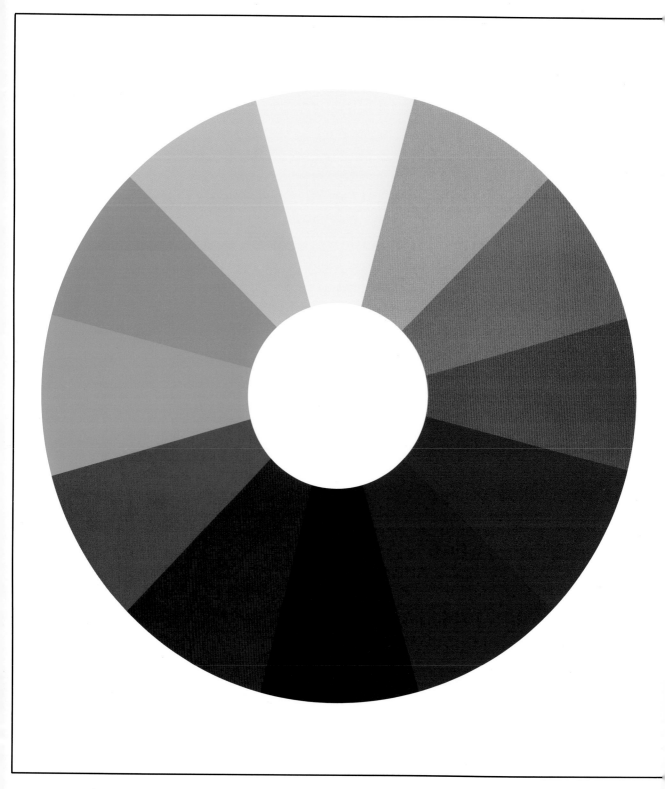

will enhance blue eyes, whilst the truth is that it overpowers them.

THE COMPLEMENTARY COLOURS ARE:
Red and Green
Blue and Orange
Yellow and Violet

In colour psychology the importance of this becomes clearer when we realize that complementary colours, when put together, present perfect balance, as all the pigment primaries are then present:

Red and (Blue + Yellow)
Blue and (Red + Yellow)
Yellow and (Red + Blue)

One of the difficulties of working with colour derives from the way the human brain is structured. It is divided into two hemispheres, separated by a strong connecting cable, called the corpus callosum. The right hemisphere governs the left side of the body, and vice versa. Linear skills, language, rationalizing and logic are driven by the left brain, while intuition, non-verbal communication – art, music, creativity – and visual information are processed by the right brain. In order to learn and appreciate colour fully the right side of the brain does most of the work, but to establish credibility and communicate it widely one must find a way of translating the knowledge into predominantly left-brain terms.

The psychology of colour works as follows: when light strikes the eye, each wavelength does so slightly differently. Red, the longest wavelength, requires the most adjustment to look at it, and therefore appears to be nearer than it is, while green requires no adjustment whatever, and is therefore restful. In the retina, these vibrations of light are converted into electrical impulses which pass to the brain – eventually to the hypothalamus, which governs the endocrine glands, which in turn produce and secrete our hormones. In simple terms each colour (wavelength) focuses on a particular part of the body, evoking a specific physiological response, which in turn produces a psychological reaction.

It seems to me that colour – light – must enter our bodies through our skin too. I cannot see how it can be limited to the eyes, although I have no scientific evidence to support the theory. There is, however, anecdotal evidence that people can differentiate colours with their eyes shut, using their fingertips. It also seems to be the case that colour blind and wholly blind people are susceptible to the psychology of colour.

It is interesting to observe how often different disciplines eventually arrive, via completely different routes, at the same point, in their search for understanding. The coming together of Eastern and Western thinking is illustrated, for example, in Western medicine's explanations of the effects of acupuncture – an ancient Chinese approach to healing, which was for

THE COLOUR WHEEL. STARTING WITH BLUE AND WORKING CLOCKWISE, YELLOW IS ADDED AND BLUE REMOVED UNTIL PURE YELLOW IS REACHED; THEN RED IS ADDED AND YELLOW REMOVED AND SO ON UNTIL THE WHEEL COMES FULL CIRCLE. THE RESULT IS THAT THE COMPLEMENTARY COLOURS LIE OPPOSITE EACH OTHER: VIOLET (RED + BLUE) OPPOSITE YELLOW; ORANGE (RED + YELLOW) OPPOSITE BLUE; AND GREEN (YELLOW + BLUE) OPPOSITE RED. EACH COMBINATION CONTAINS ALL THREE PRIMARY PIGMENTS, REPRESENTING PERFECT BALANCE.

centuries regarded in traditional Western medical circles as some kind of silly fad, but is now widely accepted as valid.

Colour is another case in point. Eastern mystics look at the influence of colours in terms very similar to Western views of the influence of the endocrine organs. They ascribe the seven spectral hues to the seven chakras (power points on the vertical plane, which 'open' as we evolve) and use them to make the link between the psychological, the physical and the spiritual – mind, body and spirit. There are striking similarities between the Western concept of associating red, for example, with the suprarenal glands, which activate the 'fight or flight' instinct, and the Eastern concept, which ascribes red to the root chakra, the physical plane – and basic survival (pink, a tint of red, represents the feminine principle and the survival of the species – nurturing, mother love).

Orange is associated with secondary survival considerations, warmth, shelter, food. Yellow (which Eastern philosophy associates with the pancreas) is about emotions, self esteem and creativity. Green reflects the concept of love, in the universal rather than the sexual sense; being at the centre of the spectrum, it also provides perfect balance. Blue encourages intellectual activity – sweet reason and calm, logical thought. Indigo has similar properties to blue but is deeper and more introverting. Finally, violet takes the mind to a higher level, towards spiritual awareness.

There is nothing new in that. Humanity, both Eastern and Western, has instinctively recognized it throughout history. The difficulty has always been the next step – how to apply with any degree of precision a concept whose principles are built on seven colours, when we see around us literally millions of variations.

There are only eleven basic colour terms in the English language. A computer of colours will show us up to sixteen million colours, but we only have names for eleven – black, white, red, orange, yellow, green, blue, purple, pink, brown and grey. Confusingly, we borrow terms from many walks of life – from Nature, from food and drink and so on – to describe colours such as peacock blue, burgundy, peach, cream, tan.

Furthermore, eleven is the maximum number of basic colour terms in any of the ninety-eight languages studied by the anthropologists Berlin and Kay in the 1960s. They conducted research amongst primitive tribes in remote parts of the world, and made astounding discoveries about the unanimity of colour naming right across the globe. White and black – light and dark – are always the first colours to be named, then red. Thereafter, the order of naming is always the same, even if, as in some cases, there are only two colour names in the language and it stops after black and white. Colour awareness is entirely cross-cultural.

What are the implications of this extraordinary fact? Could it be that we have not found words to describe colours because we know instinctively that colour is a universal language which speaks for itself? Or is it a reflection of our ignorance of colour – so complete that we have not even got as far as devising words for it?

To study colour psychology on the basis of only these eleven colours is to limit it to an impossible degree. To open it up and realize its full potential, it is vitally important that we become thoroughly acquainted with tonal variations. If we simply study 'red' as representative of a whole area of the human psyche, and 'blue' as reflecting another, which is the way it has so often been until now, we are denying the rich diversity of mankind, and the endless possibilities of colour psychology – rather like trying to write a symphony whilst recognizing only the seven notes of the C major scale. Indeed Newton ascribed the seven colours of the spectrum very precisely to the notes of the diatonic scale as follows: C = red; D = orange; E = yellow; F = green; G = blue; A = indigo; B = violet. But that is only the beginning; music and colour run virtually parallel in the expression of life's order and beauty, with wonderful symphonies and glorious colours. Millions of fine harmonies.

Interestingly, work has been carried out consistently throughout the last 350 years or so, attempting to perfect an instrument which will translate colour into sound and 'play' colours. Many sensitive people see musical notes as colours, a phenomenon known as synaesthesia. It can also apply to lines, letters, numbers, days of the week – all kinds of apparently disparate connections.

Nevertheless, on balance it is good news that colour has been left mainly in the realms of the right brain. Like music, that is where it belongs, and it should be allowed to express so much for which words are entirely inadequate. A friend of mine observed many years ago that the most powerful insights are pre-verbal. By the time a flash has been converted into a thought, it has already been diluted; translating it into words can lose it completely. Colour is Nature's own form of pure communication – a much more reliable form, a language which every single one of us was born understanding clearly, and which we all use every day, with varying degrees of conscious awareness, regardless of cultural division and conditioning.

In order to start developing this wonderful language, we must first revert to basic scientific thinking.

PERCEPTIONS OF COLOUR

Science recognizes four psychological primary colours – red, green, blue and yellow.

Red and its derivatives relate to the physical; it is often said that it has been proved that surrounding people with red will raise their blood pressure, but there is little academic record of any experiments confirming this; the only one I have found is described by Faber Birren, the great twentieth-century American colourist, in his book *Color Psychology and Color Therapy*, in which he refers to Robert Gerard's thesis for the University of California at Los Angeles. Birren describes experiments where Gerard used red, blue and white lights, transmitted on a diffusing screen. It seems to make sense; red certainly seems to be physically stimulating. Because it

CITY DWELLERS ARE
REFRESHED AND
RESTORED BY SPENDING
TIME AMID THE
GREENERY OF THE
COUNTRY.

requires such an adjustment in the eye, it appears to be nearer than it is, which is why it is so often used when visual impact is important. The most obvious example of our recognition that red catches the eye is its use the world over for traffic signals. Many football teams have red in their club colours, and thus create an impression of physical strength, even aggression – the other side of the same coin.

Blue is the colour of the intellect. In the same evidence about raising blood pressure with red, so blue is deemed to lower the blood pressure. Certainly it is a soothing, calming colour, encouraging reflection. Nature uses it most lavishly – in the sky and the sea – but this is in a reflective sense, as neither air nor water contains any colour.

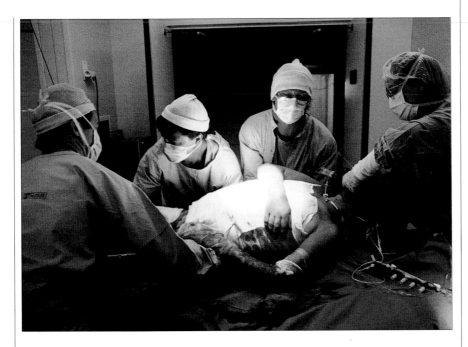

Yellow focuses on the emotions. Having learned that the third chakra relates to the pancreas, I could not at first understand the link, but then I realized – if we are nervous, where do we feel it? We have 'butterflies in our tummy'. Our stomachs churn. The solar plexus is very sensitive, and relates to the Japanese concept of the Hara (as in 'Hara Kiri') – located in the same area of the body, and perceived as the seat of all emotion. Have you ever thought about where the symbolic 'yellow streak' is located?

Green is at the centre of the spectrum and represents perfect balance. It strikes the eye at the point requiring no adjustment, thereby presenting no strain. The pigment which reflects green – chlorophyll – is vital to life, and when our environment contains plenty of green we are reassured.

Another difficulty in applying colour psychology has always been that, like everything else in the universe, there are no absolutes, only relative perceptions – so there is no such thing as a good colour or a bad colour. You may understand exactly which is the appropriate hue for a particular proposition, but it is all too easy to communicate its negative perceptions. For example, red may be stimulating and exciting or it could come across as stressful and aggressive; blue can be perceived as cold and aloof, yellow might be emotionally demanding and green could make you feel physically ill. The key to protecting positive perceptions and affective influence of any colour lies in the way it is used.

People always respond more positively to their own preferred variations of a hue than to any other. I will go further, and say that an individual will sometimes actively react against some versions of a colour, even when it is basically his or her favourite hue. So, although work on assessing people's state of mind by asking them to put sets of colours in order of preference is well established and effective, achieving a degree of accuracy, it is flawed, and possibly distorted completely, when the particular variation of the colour is not taken into account. I found this when I was tested: asked to place eight colours in order of preference, I placed the green at number seven (before black). Green is my favourite colour, but the particular cold bluish green that confronted me was a tone to which I do not ever respond. I usually prefer green to red, blue or yellow, but in this case I greatly preferred the red and the yellow, which were rich, warm tones. The person testing me refused to consider the possibility that I would have placed a different green at number one, and proceeded to give me a very distorted assessment. I was unable to recognize much of myself in what he told me. If it is the case that those variation preferences can be rationalized, and that response to the tonal family overrides response to the properties of the spectral hue, this makes a vital difference to those tests.

This point is at the root of all the difficulties in capturing the science of colour psychology, and it was often said that it was not possible, because defining it scientifically would always be countered by mankind's unpredictability and subjectivity. In 1950 Faber Birren said,

> Research on the psychological aspects of colour is difficult for the mere reason that human emotions are none too stable and the psychic make up of human beings varies from person to person.

But recognizable patterns in the psychic make up of human beings have been identified, and it is not true that they vary totally from person to person; more recently, recognizable patterns of colour have also been identified. It is therefore now possible to establish a precise relationship between the subject and the stimulus, which enables us to predict specific response, and answer the eternal question: why does one variation of a hue have such a different effect from another? Zelanski and Fisher referred to this in their book *Colour* as recently as 1989:

> Lest we hasten to repaint everything in attempts at behaviour modification, we should note that physiological color responses are complex. *The precise variation of a hue has a major impact, but one that is rarely addressed by psychological research.*

The emphasis is mine, and sums up in one sentence the essence of my work, and of this book.

So, for example, where researchers might until now have put six people in green surroundings to monitor whether green is reassuring and restful, and found that four of the six were duly reassured and rested, but the other two were not, and even felt slightly sick, this two-thirds positive response would be the published finding. I would suggest that the other two subjects should then be surrounded by a different tone of green – a tone specifically related to themselves – in order to achieve the same posi-

tive effect. I would expect, if the second experiment included all six subjects, and the alternative colours were strong enough, that the findings
would be reversed. The accuracy of all the established colour psychology
tests could be revolutionized if four different variations of the same colour
were used each time. It is not, as Faber Birren stated, the unpredictabitity
of human emotion which negates these tests, but the over-simplified definition of the colour, which fails to take account of the entirely predictable
response to different versions of the same hue.

In my early study of colour as Nature uses it, observing the seasonal
patterns and variations of the same seven spectral hues, I absorbed, almost
unconsciously, the recognition of natural harmony and its vital importance.
The question of whether or not to use blue or green, red or yellow, in any
piece of work is of secondary importance to the primary question of precisely what relationship exists among the tones. Disharmony negates.

Humans do not ever respond to one colour only, but to all the colours
presented. We have a deep need for harmony and balance, and we
instinctively respond positively to them. Indeed, we are in many ways naturally designed to restore balance whenever we are confronted by any
kind of imbalance. For example, when the eye has been focused on one
colour for more than thirty seconds or so and then closes, or looks away,
an after-image immediately presents itself in the complementary colour.
This restores the balance in the eye. One practical application of this phenomenon is the effectiveness of using green in operating theatres; when a
surgeon looks up from the patient, where he or she may have been working with the inevitable predominance of blood red for some time, the
green rests the eyes. The current trend towards a cold, light blue for theatre gowns is reasonably accurate psychologically, in terms of centring the
mind and supporting efficiency, but it takes no account of the visual strain
described, and so I question whether it is as effective overall as green.

Projecting the positive perceptions of any colour we wish to use is a
matter of understanding its tonal family, rather than considering only the
basic properties of the hue. This presents us with a more objective
approach to colour harmony and its psychology – a measurable scientific
reality, not something lost in the mists of human unpredictability, about
which we should merely shrug. This is a clearly predictable phenomenon,
a tool which we can use to influence our own moods, as well as reading
others', and to present accurately the most positive aspect of anything to
all people, across social and cultural boundaries.

CHAPTER THREE

The Natural Order

I had the great good fortune to find a wonderful teacher in California, and the first thing she encouraged me to do was often to walk the Pacific shoreline and the countryside of Carmel Valley, just to observe and soak up the colours of the natural world. I saw countless different colours of sand, from almost silver-white through myriad tones of golden brown to virtually blue-black. I noted that the green leaves of every flower were exactly the right tone of green to enhance most the colour of the petals. How many greens are there in the grass? I had never realized before how unaware I was of flowers, until we noticed how often my teacher mentioned them to demonstrate a point, and I was unfamiliar with the flower in question. This reached ridiculous proportions one day, when I said to her,

'What is the flower we see so much of around here – I have seen them in England too? It is rather a rough-looking bloom, and it comes in blue, purple or pink. It is quite tall and spindly, not at all luxuriant.'

She had no idea. She asked me a few questions about it, but eventually we decided that I should bring one in for her to see. The next day, I brought her a bunch of them, and she laughed aloud:

'You don't know a cornflower when you see one?'

I had often described eyes as 'cornflower blue' without having the least idea what a cornflower looked like

Allowing myself to open up to the natural world introduced me to the way Nature uses colour as a communication system; for so long I had taken it for granted, as most of us do. We rely on the colours in vegetables to tell us if they are good to eat; we know when the world about us turns grey that it is time to draw in and prepare for winter. When the landscape is very green, we recognize that this indicates plenty of water, and therefore little danger of famine – we are instinctively reassured. In the animal kingdom we know that any strongly coloured black and yellow creature is unlikely to be friendly.

It was this teacher who drew my attention to the different moods of Nature, and how clearly she expresses herself – at different times of the day, in different seasons of the year. In the course of one year, we see her completely change her apparel, and with it her entire personality. In California, the four seasons are not so spectacularly defined as in Europe, but even so, no one needs a watch to know if it is dawn or dusk, nor a calendar to recognize spring or autumn. The natural world holds all the answers and, although we can never completely recreate Nature's matchless harmonies, we can learn from them.

Consider the natural order: if we go out into the countryside in the springtime and look at Nature – not in city parks, or garden centres, where humans have interfered, but right out into the wild – we see literally millions of colours, and they all harmonize perfectly. But we do not need to be told that it is spring, nor in fact do we need to look at the colours. A blind man knows that it is spring when he is in the country. You can feel it in the air; there is a sense of rebirth, the return of light and warmth. Nature is very busy, the birds make a lot of noise and everything is full of water, sparkling, as the ice cracks and the snow melts. Spirits lift and we instinctively join in to celebrate the end of winter's long, cold, dark months.

As the year progresses, the earth begins to dry out and the atmosphere changes. Cool becomes attractive, and everything softens as Nature sits back and gracefully allows all the high-energy work of the springtime to take its course. The green of the leaves loses its brightness, as they tone down and match the soft colours of the summer flowers. Roses, sweet peas and wistaria have a completely different quality from the bright perkiness of spring blooms – daffodils, crocuses and bluebells.

If we go back to that same place in the country in the autumn, again we see millions of colours, and again we see perfect harmony. But it is a completely different colour scheme and a completely different atmosphere. Nature's mood has changed; her personality in the autumn is rich and abundant. It is not a particularly flowery time of year; there is flamboyance and drama in the leaves as they turn from green through yellows, golds, reds and purples and finally brown, before they fall to the ground. Autumn is the completion of the natural cycle, and presents a last blaze of defiance before everything dies down.

Then suddenly it has all gone, and we see the awesome grandeur of the winter landscape. In wintertime everything retreats under the surface, to hibernate and gather strength. The surface is minimal, and innately dramatic. Imagine a snow-covered field – a broad expanse of unbroken white, then the sharp outline of an apparently black tree trunk, with its leafless branches etched against an icy sky; the sudden drama of a holly bush. Or shadows lengthening over mountain peaks in the Alps, as night falls. We tend to treat Nature with particular respect in winter. Most of the time it is hushed – unless a storm breaks out, when we instinctively run for cover.

In Britain, and in much of Europe and North America, the four seasons are a particularly clear manifestation of the natural order, and Nature does not confuse us by, for example, producing daffodils in autumn – daffodils simply do not harmonize with chrysanthemums – or shedding the leaves from the trees in the middle of summer.

But there is no need to wait a whole year to watch the patterns unfold; each day is a microcosm of the same process. Sunrise, when the air is clear and the colours delicate, heralds a new beginning; noon, at the zenith of the day, is when the inclination is to ease off and relax; at

ABOVE: FORGET YOUR IDEAS OF HOT, VIVID SUMMER COLOURS – THIS COOL BLUE MEADOW CAPTURES PERFECTLY NATURE'S HAZY GENTLENESS WHEN THE SUN BEATS DOWN AND BLEACHES EVERYTHING OUT.

LEFT: THIS LITTLE FELLOW MAY SCURRY AWAY SHYLY FROM YOUR FEET, BUT IN THE WILD HE IS AN AGGRESSIVE PREDATOR. HIS COLOURING IS A WARNING TO HIS PREY.

LEFT: IN SPRING NATURE IS REBORN – SPIRITS LIFT AS LIGHT AND WARMTH RETURN.

THE AWE-INSPIRING
GRANDEUR OF THE
WINTER LANDSCAPE

AUTUMN — A LAST BLAZE
OF DEFIANCE BEFORE
THE RETRENCHMENT
OF WINTER.

sunset, when the cycle is nearing completion, the fading day produces dramatic, fiery colours as Nature prepares to go under cover until the next new beginning. Finally comes night – the time for hibernation and regeneration, when the velvet indigo sky is dramatically highlighted by the silver moon and stars.

The play of light and its colours creates these different pictures, and every living creature on earth responds instinctively to their messages and acts accordingly. We depend on this natural order at a very primitive level.

I am indebted to the colourists of Northern California in the 1950s and 1960s (although some of their principles have been considerably diluted, if not discarded altogether, by more recent practitioners, working mainly in the field of fashion and beauty) for first beginning to recognize that humanity's place in the Grand Design is clearly identifiable when we realize that we too echo these same patterns, and the physical colouring and personality of each individual reflects the pattern to which he or she is linked. It has nothing to do with seasons in the context of time – the time of year when you were born is not relevant – but in the context of identification and orientation.

I mentioned in Chapter One that I would introduce more poetic names for the four types. I am not the first to use the seasonal association; it is a very descriptive way of helping people to envisage readily, and understand clearly, the essential qualities of each type. I propose therefore to refer to Type I personalities and Group I colours as Spring-linked, Type II and Group II as Summer-linked, Type III and Group III as autumnal and Type IV and Group IV as Winter-linked.

People reflecting the patterns of spring are warm, light and friendly extroverts. Outgoing and gregarious, they are excellent communicators, but not at their best when confronted by anything 'heavy' or deep. They have a strong instinctive need for plenty of light.

Summer-linked personalities are more contained. Cool, calm and collected, they are understated and crave order and balance. They do not find it necessary to comment on everything, but miss very little, as they are perceptive and often highly intelligent.

The third type of person is much more fiery and intense. These autumnal people get very involved in situations and have inquiring minds; they question everything – mainly because they reject anything which might be invalid, flimsy or insubstantial. Substance is more important to them than style, so they are initially sceptical, but once convinced will commit themselves passionately.

The fourth group are those people whom one instinctively tends to treat with respect; they do not need to indulge in tantrums or create drama because it is an innate quality in them. They are perfectionists, efficient and forward thinking, and they do not suffer fools gladly. They need a sense of space. They echo the characteristics of winter.

Surrounding yourself with colours which are at odds with your own natural pattern, vibrating on different frequencies from your own, is in the long run a stressful thing to do. For example, a richly warm, dramatic and extroverted brunette wearing cold, introverting black is essentially under a strain – and it usually shows; women tend to compensate for this with extra make-up, which can compound the problem. Another frequently observed strain is when a naturally intense, fiery woman bleaches all the richness out of her hair and dyes it 'baby blonde', adopts the habit of sweet pink lipstick and nail polish, and expects the world to believe that she is Bo Peep. This is usually an indication that she is afraid to show her power, but the only one she is fooling is herself. When the bleached hair is also cropped almost to the scalp, there are issues of the power of femininity. People are often uncomfortable around a woman who is putting herself and them through this. Authenticity is universally attractive, and most people have a strong inbuilt mechanism for registering when it is absent. We may not be able to identify what it is that does not feel quite right, but we are not comfortable. Pretending to be something we are not, and vice versa, is exhausting.

A common example of a similar misuse of colour is very apparent if you visit the home of someone who has left himself out of the equation when decorating. Slavishly copying the 'fashionable' colours in style magazines, or commissioning interior designers who do not take enough trouble to understand you and your needs, but prefer to create a reputation for themselves, results in homes where everything is apparently wonderful, but for some reason you cannot put your finger on, it is uncomfortable. It just does not feel right. Such an atmosphere does not support happiness and harmony, and nobody, except perhaps the designer, wants to spend more time there than is necessary.

CHAPTER FOUR

Colour Science

As I explained in Chapter Two, simultaneously with attempting to identify the links between precise tonal variations of each hue and fine nuances of human emotion, it is essential to identify the physical qualities that differentiate the four tonal families of colour, and learn to recognize them. Take one spectral hue – yellow. What is the difference between a Spring yellow – daffodils – and an Autumn yellow – chrysanthemums (and new yellow dusters) – given that they are both warm? And how is a cold – lemon – yellow achieved?

While we have a long way to go yet, with the aid of sophisticated colour computers, before we can classify all shades, tones and tints completely 'by numbers', we have made considerable progress. For instance, the answers to the above questions appear to be that Spring colours do not contain any black, and only go to certain levels of saturation. In the Scandinavian Institute's Natural Colour System – known as the NCS – pure yellow, added to white in increments of 5 per cent, belongs in the Spring family until it gets to 70 per cent when the intensity becomes Autumnal. The addition of any black or red instantly takes pure yellow into the Autumn spectrum. Winter yellow has a touch of green added – not more than 30 per cent; after that it becomes a warm green – and Summer yellows (of which there are not many) have a hint of both green and grey. When a greenish blue becomes a bluish green (i.e. as more green is added) it passes from Autumn to Winter.

I await with great eagerness the day when the tracking of colours around a horizontal circular axis from yellow through red, blue and green back to yellow again, and up and down the vertical black/white axis is completed, and we can see exactly what physical characteristics the colours in one season, or tonal family, share. We are working on it.

Meanwhile, there is a very specific and unmistakable harmony that comes into play when colours of the same family are put together. Recognizing that harmony is something one can be trained to do, though many people recognize it without any training whatever. So, once you have one colour which you know belongs to a particular season, you can then classify whether any other colour belongs to the same season by putting them together and observing the relationship between them.

For the purpose of this book, we can draw upon traditional visual means to demonstrate the characteristics that colours in each of the four groups share. It is obviously not possible to attempt a complete analysis of every colour, but a representative palette will demonstrate the points surprisingly clearly.

Look at the palettes on the following pages: each of them contains a selection of sixteen colours. They are, in one sense, the same sixteen, but the tonal variations are different. Look at them quite separately, if you want to gauge your own psychological response to each.

Every shade, tone or tint falls into only one palette – there is no such thing as a colour which is common to more than one season. However, three colours which are very balanced, and occur close to the centre of the seasonal spectra, are turquoise, peach and cream (or off white) – all strictly speaking Spring colours. Given that we are rarely presented with a completely free hand, they can in certain cases cross the seasons to accommodate practicalities and reconcile disparate colour schemes.

THE SPRING PALETTE

Palette number one relates to the springtime. The colours are warm and essentially light – tints. Clarity is at the heart of this pattern, and there are virtually primary colours to be found there. The sort of names we use to describe them are scarlet, coral, watermelon, peach, sunshine yellow, emerald green, apple, aquamarine, turquoise, cobalt blue, sky blue, lilac, violet. The neutrals which support these colours are cream, camel and light grey.

There are no dark colours in this palette. Even the 'navy' blues are relatively bright and warm, with little relevance to a naval uniform, which is virtually black. There are greys, but again they have a warmth and a buoyancy about them which is supportive of these delicate, clear colours, rather than suppressive. Contemplating this palette, whether personally identified with it or not, one can instinctively sense the liveliness, the sparkle and the simplicity.

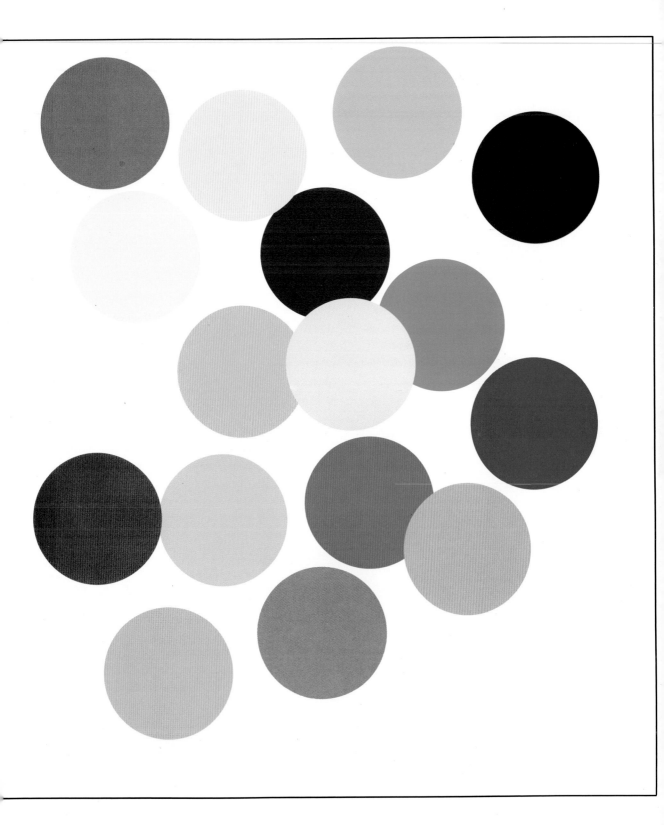

THE SUMMER PALETTE

Palette number two has a different quality. These colours are virtually all tones – they have a high percentage of grey in them – and there are no clear primary colours. Subtlety is the keynote here. Colour names for this tonal family include: maroon, shell pink, rose pink, ashes of roses, plum, grapefruit, sage green, veridian, bottle green, powder blue, Royal Air Force blue, lavender, mauve. Supportive neutrals include taupe, cool navy, mid grey and oyster.

There are no extremes in the Summer palette. If you were to study a colour atlas, you would find all the Summer tones falling near the middle. Again, they are light, but in this case it is light in weight – some of the colours are quite dark, but they are never heavy, always subtle and delicate.

The characteristics expressed in the Summer palette are cool and calm, elegant, graceful, understated.

THE AUTUMN PALETTE

With the third palette we find again warm colours and a certain amount of liveliness. This time, however, there is more intensity and the colours are mainly shades – by no means primary. They are off beat, and vary between flamboyant strength and extreme subtlety. Names for these shades include vermilion, poppy, flame, burnt orange, rust, mustard, butter yellow, leaf green, olive green, forest green, teal blue, peacock, petrel, aubergine, warm burgundy. The best neutrals are all warm browns – from light stone through tobacco to dark chocolate.

In printing, it is possible to achieve Autumn 'navy' blues and grey. In fashion, it rarely happens; the dark blues produced by fabric dyes do not have the warmth of Autumn until they contain enough green to become the shades described as teal blue or petrel. Pure grey does not feature in an autumnal palette; the nearest we get to it is strictly speaking either a green or a stone beige – more readily achievable with printing inks.

The associations these colours have are with the earth, the natural world. Implicit in this palette are depth and substance, rich abundance and maturity.

THE WINTER PALETTE

Finally, the fourth palette contains very strong primary colours – strong contrasts between pure hues, extreme tints and extreme shades, but no tones. You will notice that this is the only one which includes pure white and black. The names applied here include magenta, crimson, pillar-box red, shocking pink, Persian orange (a cold orange is almost – but not quite – a contradiction in terms. This a very specific tone which is not seen often, but does enjoy popularity in fashion from time to time), lemon yellow, pistachio, jade green, crème de menthe, cyan, royal blue, ice blue, midnight blue, indigo, royal purple. Supportive neutrals are black, white, charcoal or silver grey and navy (much nearer to a naval uniform) – no creams, beiges or other subtle tones.

Contemplating this palette, one is aware of the implicit drama and sophistication it contains. There are no subtleties here, but crystal clarity and power.

PART TWO

YOUR PERSONAL PALETTE

IT IS WORTH QUOTING THE GIFTED AMERICAN COLOURIST, SUZANNE CAYGILL, WHO WROTE A BOOK IN 1980 CALLED COLOR – THE ESSENCE OF YOU. ON THE BACK COVER SHE SAYS:

THE SOURCE OF ALL COLOR IS NATURE. IF WE BECOME AWARE THAT NATURE HAS PROVIDED US WITH A SET OF COLOR CLUES, OR STANDARDS, AND IF WE ARE ABLE TO PICK THEM UP, IT WILL BE POSSIBLE TO USE THESE STANDARDS IN THE SEARCH FOR SELF.

CHAPTER FIVE

Identify Your True Colours

The struggle to make sense of this life, and one's own place in it, to learn its lessons and make some progress towards enlightenment, is a very strange process. We go around in circles, learning the esoteric catchphrases: 'Don't give away your power'; 'Love yourself'; 'Go inside yourself to find the answers'; 'You create your own reality'; 'Surrender to your Higher Self' and thoroughly agreeing with every word. But nothing changes, and life goes on happening to us. Why? Will endlessly talking about ourselves and intellectualizing about these concepts eventually pay off?

Something more is required, a kind of translation tool. Colour psychology can provide the bridge between academic understanding and truly knowing ourselves, independently of what we have been conditioned to believe about ourselves and society by well-meaning parents and other guiding influences, almost from the moment we were born. Everyone comes to wisdom and understanding in his own way. Some people are born with a level of spiritual awareness which enables them to get straight into the far reaches of metaphysics, but most start with the mundane questions relating to everyday concerns of personal presentation, relationships, career – just getting through life.

The approach to colour psychology contained in this book presents a clear and relatively easy crossing into the field of vision in which we can begin to understand ourselves more clearly, and recognize our place in the greater scheme of things. To start on the simple everyday level of 'What colour lipstick suits me?' is just fine. The answer to that question is the first step to recognition of your own uniquely individual nature, which you can then explore at your own pace by becoming more and more aware of the colours in your personal palette.

If we consider again the natural world, we see every single plant, bird, animal or insect knowing precisely what it is and putting all its energy into simply being itself. Roses do not try to look or be more like oak trees; sheep do not paint stripes on themselves and pretend they are tigers; tigers don't tell the world they are deer. We, mankind, supposedly more evolved and of a higher intelligence than anything else, are the only ones who play those games, and mankind is, generally speaking, the only species which is deeply unhappy.

We are all searching for an understanding of self, but we obscure and distort it before we have even begun if we allow the opinions and perceptions of others to eclipse our own unique view, and determine how we should present ourselves to the rest of the world. Sadly, this is exactly what most people do.

SO WHAT TYPE AM I?

No doubt your response to all this is leading you to wonder about your own pattern, and I propose to devote some time to that question, provided it is clearly understood that there are limits to how complete a character analysis is possible in a book of this kind. When people first read descriptions classifying each person according to a season of the year, they naturally try to identify themselves, and often find themselves unable to do so; they become very confused, seeing aspects of themselves reflected in all four patterns described.

Although you are unlikely to acquire a complete picture of yourself, with all your quirks, just from reading any book, nevertheless you will gain some interesting insights. Do remember Suzanne's words, and also bear in mind that, at this stage, we are only identifying archetypes. It is worth remembering, too, if you want to type yourself accurately, that everyone aspires to be glamorous, self-assured Winter, but the incidence of this type in the West is not high. Do not jump to the wishful conclusion that this is you. If it is, your nature is such that you know it anyway, and are less likely to attach too much importance to the following in confirming your view of yourself.

It might be interesting for you to begin establishing your own pattern by deciding to which of the four pages of colour in the previous chapter you responded most positively. Don't give it too much thought – trust your first, instinctive response. It is not necessarily the case that this preference test will define your own seasonal orientation absolutely, but it does for, say, 70–80 per cent of people. The rest may have strong subordinate influences pulling them, or there can be other reasons, so for the moment just note the preference. It might be that you are torn between two – in this case one of them is probably your true season and the other a strong subordinate influence. The question of subordinate influences will be explained in Chapter Six.

The search for self in adulthood is rather like peeling an onion, as we work our way through layer after layer of conditioning. The colours you wear in your clothing are less likely to be an accurate expression of yourself than the colours you prefer for your home, your jewellery, pictures and other expressions less susceptible to fashion. The conditioning in fashion is very strong but essentially ephemeral, so for the moment let us ignore the outer layers of the onion and concentrate on truer indications of the real person. Try the following questionnaire:

1. Excluding black and white, what is your favourite primary colour?

a. Yellow

b. Blue

c. Green

d. Red

2. In choosing a home, would you say your most important consideration (after location, price and other practical matters) was:

a. Light

b. Proportion

c. Substance

d. Space

3. Given a free hand and no budgetary restraints, which of the following best describes the sitting room you would ideally design for yourself?

a. A bright, airy room, with French windows leading to the garden, and plenty of living green plants – ferns, palms or flowering; the predominant colours are peach, sea blue or champagne, with touches of green or yellow; there is a floral pattern, either in the upholstery or in the curtains, and considerable thought has gone into the latter – they are ruched or frilled in some way; lots of blonde wood, such as pine or ash – possibly wicker or cane. There is a slight sense of bringing the garden into the room. The atmosphere is informal, and there are plenty of ornaments and mementoes on display.

b. A graceful, high-ceilinged room furnished with exquisite antiques having curved, delicate lines; fine quality carpeting or perhaps a polished parquet floor and Chinese carpets or rugs. Colours are soft grey, blues, rosy pinks; curtains are flowing silk moire, elegantly designed and with net or chiffon inner curtains. There are expensive vases here and there containing freshly cut flowers, and the whole atmosphere is one of calm order – current issues of magazines in the canterbury; no clutter. This is gracious living.

c. A room whose focal point is the fireplace – inglenook, brick or stone – with an oak mantel. The floor is varnished boards strewn with Persian or Turkish rugs, or it is carpeted in thick Berber. There is a big rubber plant and several dark green plants dotted around – all flourishing – and bookshelves line at least one wall. The seating consists mainly of large, squashy armchairs and sofas and there is emphasis on richly toned timber – possibly beams or a large coffee table. Curtains are muslin or linen, dupion or other textured fabric. The main colour scheme is neutral honey or beige tones, and there are dramatically hued cushions in fiery reds, orange, rust, or vivid peacock blues. The atmosphere is of solid comfort.

d. A stunningly simple room, mainly white but with touches of matt black in the furniture. There is glass, either in the heavy plate glass and chrome coffee table or in a large mirrored area, if not both.

THE LARGE WINDOWS, THE ROUND SHAPES, THE FLOWERING PLANTS AND THE WARM COLOURS IN THIS ROOM CREATE A PERFECT ENVIRONMENT FOR A SPRING PERSONALITY.

THIS STARKLY DRAMATIC ROOM WILL APPEAL TO THE WINTER PERSONALITY. THE VIVID YELLOW CUSHIONS ARE A TYPICAL WINTER TOUCH.

It is minimally furnished, but everything is extremely expensive and dramatically avant garde; the upholstery may be black leather and windows are dressed with blinds rather than curtains. The main colour scheme is achromatic, but there are dramatic accents of vivid red, jade green or lemon yellow. There are no floral decorations, but striking small modern sculptures instead. The atmosphere is impressive and futuristic – the Bauhaus school of thought.

RIGHT: THE CLASSIC GLAMOUR OF THIS DIAMOND NECKLACE WOULD ONLY BE PERFECTLY SET OFF BY THE DRAMATIC COLOURING AND PERSONALITY OF A WINTER WOMAN.

FAR RIGHT: A TYPICAL AUTUMN WOMAN WOULD LOVE THIS INSPIRED SETTING OF PREDOMINANTLY SEMI-PRECIOUS GEMS IN HEAVY GOLD.

4. Irrespective of price or status, what kind of jewellery appeals to you?

a. Light gold filigree, yellow sapphires, emeralds, opals

b. Platinum or white gold, moonstones, tourmalines, a star sapphire, classic pearls

c. Chunky gold, copper or brass, ethnic style, topaz, amber, garnets, a fire opal

d. Silver, unusual setting, diamonds, rubies, black pearls, jet

5. What is your favourite kind of social event?

a. A picnic, a musical or the circus; spontaneous parties

b. Concerts or the ballet; an elegant dinner party

c. The opera, the cinema or a meaty courtroom drama; evenings by the fire with close friends

d. A fashionable cocktail party, first nights, art house cinema, a book launch

6. Would you describe yourself as:

a. Friendly and caring

b. Rather shy

c. Interested in people

d. Confident

7. What kind of music do you like?

a.. Pop, rock'n'roll, operetta or light classical

b. Tschaikowski, Mozart, Bach, Schubert

c. Opera, heavy rock, folk, Beethoven

d. Jazz, contemporary classical, heavy metal, Gorecki

8. In art, regardless of your education, would you instinctively gravitate most towards:

a. Watercolours

b. Impressionism

c. Oil paintings

d. Etchings or line drawing

9. When you consider the concept of leadership, would you, as a leader:

a. Motivate others with your enthusiasm

b. Really prefer to be the 'power behind the throne'

c. Lead from the front, never asking others to do anything which you are not prepared to do yourself

d. Take an overview, and concentrate on the most effective delegation

10. A group of you are gathered for a social occasion, when the hostess announces that the event is in jeopardy because the babysitter has just phoned to say she cannot come, and can anyone find another babysitter at such short notice. Would you:

a. Remembering that your aunt's best friend knew a treasure of a babysitter five years ago, set about trying to locate this paragon

b. Simply consult your neat notebook of useful information and find the perfect solution

c. Spend considerable time and energy on how and why the babysitter could be so unreliable, before addressing the problem and probably solving it

d. Be unlikely to register the question

A word about question 1. The colour associated with each season is related to the essence of the archetypal personality, but blue is the most widely held favourite colour, worldwide, and many people respond strongly to the colour of their own eyes, so if, for example, you feel you are linked to Spring but your favourite colour is blue, do not be put off. Only if you actively dislike yellow should you perhaps think again.

If you have answered mostly **a**., and your preference was for palette number one, then you either are linked to the Spring patterns, or you have considerable influence of Spring in you. You probably are Spring, and fairly well in tune with yourself.

The same can be said if you answered mainly **b**. and preferred palette number two, but here the leaning is towards Summer.

Mostly **c**. answers and a preference for palette number three reflect the autumnal pattern. Mostly **d**. answers and palette number four indicate Winter's expressions.

Most people will be beginning to have a fairly clear idea by now of their own pattern, but there could be complications. If, for example, most of your answers in the questionnaire relate to one season, but you strongly prefer the picture presented by a different palette, this might indicate that you are denying your true nature – or simply that you have lost sight of yourself. It might be that your self-esteem is low and you cannot see the beauty in your own pattern, but prefer a picture of someone else.

If your answers in the questionnaire were not predominantly one pattern, it may simply be that you do not know yourself very well.

It is probably not a bad idea, if you are in either of these situations, to solicit the opinions of someone who knows you really well and loves you. Husbands are often extraordinarily perceptive about their wives' colour patterns, but oddly, when the situation is reversed, wives seem less able to see their husbands objectively, and are prone to imposing their own patterns. (How often have you seen them together in the Menswear Dept!)

Unless you are really confused, however, it is better not to seek anyone else's opinion. The truth of the matter is that you were born knowing and understanding yourself perfectly and the only reason you need to read this book and examine these questions is to remind yourself of who you really are, so that you can get back on to your own unique path, from which other people's opinions and conditioning may have led you to stray.

At the same time, I am often amazed at the misconceptions we have about ourselves. I am sure we can all cite examples of people who constantly tell us what their own characteristics are (often in the process of criticizing others) whilst their behaviour demonstrates the exact opposite.

Now that you are beginning to recognize your own type, it is worth examining in more depth the implications of this personality typing, and how to use it. Whenever people ask me what type I think they are, I always reply that I do not know. There are two reasons for this: firstly, without a proper consultation I really do *not* know; although I might make an educated guess at the predominant season, I would be unlikely to identify subordinate influences fully; secondly, such an oversimplification will not do them any favours. If I tell someone that he or she is 'linked to Spring' without spending time explaining further what exactly that means, and how to use the information, this is at best meaningless and at worst quite harmful, if it presents them with another label, which they do not understand but still attach to themselves and try to accommodate.

Before going any further, let us review what we have established so far about the four archetypes:

SPRING

Your guiding element is water (preferably moving). You are a light, warm, outgoing person, friendly and caring; you like yellow, and have a deep need for plenty of light in your life. You do not stand on ceremony. Your ideal sitting room has French windows, plenty of pot plants, an informal atmosphere and a sense of bringing the garden indoors. You like sparkling jewellery, gold-based, with yellow sapphires, emeralds or opals, and when you socialize, you like a musical show, a circus, or any informal event involving lots of people simply having fun. You like pop music, or light classics, and watercolours.

If you are successful in your job, and reach a position of leadership, you work on the basis of motivating subordinates with your enthusiasm – indeed, enthusiasm is a key characteristic of yours. You will go to endless trouble to help, but sometimes your enthusiasm can run away with you (unless you have a streak of Winter efficiency running through you). You are witty and charming and communicate well – your natural talents will shine if you work in the media, or in sales and marketing. You might make a wonderful nurse, as you light up people's lives with your sunny disposition and your caring attitude.

This is probably as good a point as any to remind you, however, that all characteristics can be perceived negatively. There is a danger with Spring that you can skim too lightly across life's surface; any negative perceptions of you derive from your reluctance to go out of your depth. Spring-linked men can be dreadful philanderers without meaning to mislead, and often, when the going gets rough, Spring of either sex will switch on their irresistible charm, or resort to manipulative tricks, to avoid 'heavy' situations or direct confrontation. Obviously we do not wish to dwell on negative characteristics at all, but – as mentioned earlier – there are no absolutes, and each of the four types can be perceived negatively. It is as well to understand the whole picture.

SUMMER

Your guiding element is air. You are quiet and gentle, rather shy but basically cool, calm and collected. Your favourite colour is blue and you prefer to keep things in proportion, both literally, as in your ideal room, and in psychological terms. Your jewellery is likely to be platinum or

SOME FAMILIAR PERSONALITIES WHO APPEAR TO DEMONSTRATE THE CHARACTERISTICS OF SPRING ARE:

MEG RYAN
NICHOLAS PARSONS
ELAINE PAIGE
BILL CLINTON
GOLDIE HAWN
LARRY HAGMAN
MARILYN MONROE
TOMMY STEELE
OLIVIA NEWTON JOHN
CRAIG McLAGHLAN

THE SUMMER
PERSONALITY – FOR
REASONS ALREADY
EXPLAINED – DOES NOT
DOMINATE THE PUBLIC
STAGE, BUT THE
FOLLOWING DO APPEAR
TO RELATE TO THE
PATTERN:

HM THE QUEEN
HM QUEEN ELIZABETH
THE QUEEN MOTHER
HRH THE PRINCE OF
WALES
PRINCESS GRACE OF
MONACO
NELSON MANDELA
GRETA GARBO
SIR DAVID STEELE
GARY COOPER

white gold (if the truth be told, you think yellow gold is rather vulgar), set with moonstones or tourmalines; the lustrous classic pearl necklace was invented for you. You abhor anything vulgar or flashy, and surround yourself with timeless elegance. Your socializing has a formal quality; you like classical music and love the ballet. The subtlety of impressionist painting appeals to you.

You have no wish for the limelight, and prefer to work quietly behind the scenes, where your strong nurturing instinct can sustain and balance the whole enterprise – whatever it may be. You are artistically gifted in some way. You would be wonderful running an art gallery or an antique shop or bringing your soothing diplomatic skills to bear on a career as a lawyer or as a personnel manager. The medical profession is also an appropriate arena for you.

There are a few negative perceptions of Summer, deriving from your introversion and your sense of proportion. When there is trouble, you are a natural peacemaker, and your gentle sympathy is very soothing – but you have a core of objectivity which prevents you from being drawn too far into other people's dramas, and you can often remain detached and cool to the point of seeming aloof. You might also be seen by some as rather snobbish.

The list on the left helps to demonstrate the point that Summer personalities tend not to seek the limelight, other than as an inevitable by-product of something else they are trying to achieve. In the case of the British Royal family – a family which was thrust on to the world stage by circumstances of birth – summer predominates, and Summer's typical seriousness and sense of responsibility – which has sometimes exposed them to ridicule – has actually stood them (and the country) in good stead over the last sixty years or so.

AUTUMN

Your guiding element is fire. You are essentially externally motivated, being eternally interested in people, and concepts of 'how' and 'why'. You are attracted to green and your ideal home environment will reflect the abundance and richness of the natural world. Although you are strongly influenced by other people, you like your home to be cosy and enclosed – you could happily live in the depths of the forest – but everyone is welcome to visit you.

You are not mad about precious gems, but prefer more interesting designs using semi-precious stones. Social events are often quite intense and you love a philosophical debate; strong music and rich oil paintings appeal, and your insatiable curiosity will drive you always to lead others from the front. You are efficient and strong, but often complicate matters unnecessarily with judgemental attitudes and emotion.

The negative perceptions of your personality derive from these attitudes and your fiery passion; you may be seen as bossy or rebellious, when you think that all you are trying to do is put right a wrong. Your intensity can

CELEBRITIES WHO
APPEAR TO
DEMONSTRATE AUTUMN
CHARACTERISTICS ARE:

EMMA THOMPSON
ROBERT REDFORD
DIANA RIGG
BILL COSBY
TINA TURNER
PLACIDO DOMINGO
GLENDA JACKSON
DAVID FROST
GERMAINE GREER
CLINT EASTWOOD

be exhausting. A career as a mining engineer, an investigative journalist, a psychologist or anything that takes you into the depths would be good for you. You are a wonderful campaigner, always ready to champion the underdog. (Be careful, if you decide to become a barrister, to keep a grip on your objectivity and accept that law is not necessarily always at one with justice.)

WINTER

Your guiding element is earth. You are intense and strong, but not at all externally motivated – you are quite 'centred'. You cannot stand clutter and need a sense of space. Your ideal living area will be impressively designed, and you have a well-developed instinct for the most stylish presentation. You are an arbiter of fashion, rather than a follower, and you are hedonistic, rejecting anything cheap and shoddy. You will keep jewellery to one spectacular piece, and your preference is for diamonds or rubies. A distinctive setting will appeal.

You prefer to be in the vanguard of society, and are unlikely to be found in any squalid enterprise or position of subservience – unless it suits your long-term objectives for the moment, in which case you will demonstrate great stoicism. You are completely self-assured. You enjoy experimental design, modern music, etchings.

You are a born leader, with your ability to remain detached and objective, never letting sentiment obscure the greater good, and you do not waste time on academic questions. You shine in the world of finance or politics, or you might prefer to bring your star quality to bear on the catwalk, or films, TV or theatre.

Of course, others might see you as cold and arrogant; they do not realize that you probably really do know best and your pragmatism is what will get things done. Few understand the difference between unsentimental and uncaring, but it is worth your giving that distinction some thought, if you do not want to find yourself in the position of being respected and admired, but not greatly loved.

There is a story – possibly apocryphal – which highlights perfectly the difference between Autumn and Winter. When Laurence Olivier and Dustin Hoffman worked together on the film *Marathon Man*, the former was most concerned one Monday morning, when his co-star staggered in, looking quite dreadful.

'My dear fellow!' said the noble Thespian (Lord Olivier was Winter-linked). 'You look ghastly – whatever's the matter?'

Dustin Hoffman (Autumn-linked) wearily replied, 'Oh, it's all right, Larry; it's just that I've spent the weekend getting into the part – I haven't slept for three nights.'

Olivier was genuinely bewildered: 'Have you ever thought of – er, well – acting it?'

WINTER-LINKED PERSONALITIES ARE EVERYWHERE IN THE PUBLIC EYE:

ELIZABETH TAYLOR
PAUL NEWMAN
MARGARET THATCHER
CARY GRANT
JACQUELINE KENNEDY ONASSIS
LIONEL RICHIE
CHER
JOHN TRAVOLTA
DIANA ROSS
DAVID OWEN

One way of highlighting the characteristics of the four personality types is to imagine a glossy magazine. Ideally, the advertising department will be run and staffed by Spring personalities, who could sell suntan lotion in Siberia. The Summer personalities will be running the administration department, making sure the advertising orders are properly executed, and that the invoices for them go out and are paid. Autumn personalities will be the journalists and feature writers and Winter will be the Art Director, and probably the Editor too.

This magazine analogy is an example of perfect deployment, and one of the joys of understanding this system of psychology is in being able to recognize in practice the value of combining complementary talents. Thus Spring does not get irritated with Summer's boring questions about properly signed order forms, but appreciates the importance of someone in the organization keeping their feet on the ground, and enjoys visiting the peaceful oasis of the administration department. Summer, instead of being frustrated at Spring's insouciant attitude to paperwork, recognizes their inspired charm and amazing way with people. Autumn, instead of demanding that Winter get more passionate about particular issues which are consuming him or her, will defer to the clearer vision and instinctive knowledge of the best way to present something – and be grateful for uncompromising excellence. Winter will thank Autumn for bringing fire and passion, and thoroughly researched material, into the pages.

So often we see in the workplace that colleagues judge each other by their own standards. They want to 'jazz up' the quiet girl with the dreamy eyes in Accounts. They dismiss light, witty salesmen as airheads. They accuse the boss of being cold and uncaring. They think that the bossy woman who is trying to put right an injustice should keep quiet and mind her own business.

Rather as Bernard Shaw is reputed to have replied when a female correspondent suggested that their combined attributes – her beauty and his brains – would produce amazing children:

'No doubt, my dear, but what if we produced children with my beauty and your brains?'

We so often fail to recognize the potential benefits of putting complementary characters together, as we focus on the potential personality clashes.

TYPICAL SPRING –
LIGHT, WARM, FRIENDLY
AND OUTGOING.

CHAPTER SIX

Individual Variations

In truth, there are probably aspects of all four patterns to be found in many of us. The important point to realize is that the patterns themselves are absolute – just as there are only two gender patterns in mankind – but the variations are infinite. There are many variations within each pattern, and it is essential to address the knotty complexities of subordinate influences before one can really recognize the sublime simplicity of it all.

These colour patterns govern all our five senses, and questions of line, form, space etc. follow suit, with an almost laughably simple logic.

SPRING

Springtime is essentially concerned with the return of light and warmth. Nature is stirring, and getting the new cycle underway; there is much to be done, and the mood is buoyant and sparkling – busy. For people, the most accurate expressions of these concepts are circular or spherical shapes (like bubbles), fine, clear lines and crisp, fresh textures which will not interfere with the lightness and gaiety, or inhibit the perception of movement. Smells are flowery and delicate and the most appropriate jewellery will sparkle, and possibly move. In this context, anything heavy or dark is liable to present a negative contribution. People linked to Spring may put on excess weight (and hate it), but they still seem to retain an indefinable impression of lightness; they are light on their feet, and often dance well. Right into old age, they are eternally young. Brunettes in this pattern do occur, and obviously have dark hair, but there is no great depth of intensity in the colouring. The actress Pauline Collins typifies this variation, while Diana, Princess of Wales, represented the archetype.

The Spring personality communicates well. Often witty and attractive, they charm a wide variety of people, and never become bogged down with either bureaucracy or ponderous gravity.

SUMMER

The moderation which develops as Spring progresses into Summer calls for more subtlety. These two patterns have in common a certain delicacy and lightness of touch, but Nature is maturing, and her summertime mood is softer and more flowing than lively, youthful Spring. At first, with memories of blindingly colourful summer holidays and pictures of the Caribbean, it is difficult to understand how the patterns of Summer could possibly be described as muted or cool. Then we realize that the coolness of colours which have been bleached out to delicate pastel by the sun,

BUOYANT SPRING: THIS DARK NAVY BLUE IS ELEGANT, BUT SUPPRESSES DINAH'S PERSONALITY.

THE BRIGHT PINK IS LIVELY AND SUPPORTIVE — SHE LOOKS HEALTHIER AND MORE RELAXED.

RADIANT SPRING: BLONDES OFTEN WEAR BLACK, AND JULIE IS PRETTY ENOUGH TO GET AWAY WITH IT. SHE LOOKS SLIGHTLY TENSE, THOUGH.

SEE HOW MUCH BETTER SHE LOOKS WHEN HER EYES ARE LIT UP BY THE PERIWINKLE BLUE.

subtly curved oval shapes, flawless fabrics with a soft sheen, such as pure silk jersey or floating, drifting chiffon, and anything which contributes to a sense of serene tranquillity express the most attractive aspect of the Summer – the blessed relief of a cool, calm oasis. Imagine drifting though a rose garden in the twilight of a summer evening. Energy is best contained, rather than dissipated, when the weather is likely to be very warm. Anything brash, loud or vulgar will negate the gentle charm of Summer's most elegant face – as typified, for example, by the late Princess Grace of Monaco. Order and balance are of the utmost importance to the Summer personality, chaos upsets them more than the rest of us. They are extremely sensitive – both in the sense of intuitively recognizing the feelings of others, and in physical terms, having an exquisitely developed sense of touch; a Summer-linked person would rather die than wear a garment made of cheap fabric, and the skin will often be inclined to break out in a rash, either in times of stress or if rough sweaters or questionable metals are worn. Summer men always prefer to wear silk socks. A hint of delicate fragrance will waft gently, and jewellery will glow, rather than shine or sparkle. The elegant curve of a cabochon stone will always be preferred. Summer people are often very talented in the kind of creative endeavour which involves the fingertips – such as playing a musical instrument, or needlework – or delicate intuition, such as painting. Because of their understated approach, they are sometimes perceived as rather 'wimpish', but this is a mistake. Summer people have a core of cool, fine steel running right through them.

AUTUMN

The fiery intensity of Autumn is much more earthy. We become very aware of the earth and the natural environment in the Autumn; maturity and abundance are the keynotes of the season, and patterns are inherently more solid and substantial. Lines are beginning to square off, textures are grained and nubbly – fabrics whose interest is inherent in the weave, rather than printed on to a smooth texture (although leaf patterns and Paisley prints work for this personality). Perfumes or after-shaves are more off beat and woodsy, less flowery, and chunky, gold-based jewellery, set with semi-precious stones, such as topaz or amber, have the most appeal.

The Autumn personality tends to dig deep, enquire and analyse. They also communicate well, but are more rebellious and iconoclastic than their Spring or Summer cousins. Cold colours which put out the fire, or flimsiness in any form – literally, as in very delicate furniture and gossamer fabrics, or conceptually, in any superficiality of ideas – are anathema to the positive expression of this personality. Autumn is externally motivated and often the one most likely to lose sight of self. Fire and strength are in the nature of Autumn: these are characteristics which can get us into trouble, so denial seems more comfortable, particularly for women. The pioneering spirit is the spirit of Autumn and all the women in the vanguard of feminism, and most of the alternative comedians, are autumnal. No matter how

FLORAL SUMMER: ONE MIGHT EXPECT THIS
WARM PERIWINKLE TO BRING OUT CAROLINE'S
LOVELY BLUE EYES, BUT IT DOESN'T; SHE IS FAR
FROM RELAXED.

LOOK AT THOSE EYES NOW!

HEATHER SUMMER: NOEL'S AUTUMN SUBORDINATE
ENABLES HIM TO WEAR THESE COLOURS, BUT HE IS
UNDER A STRAIN — AND IT SHOWS.

THESE COOL TONES ARE MUCH BETTER FOR HIM.

cool and submissive the surface, that fire is there, and it is better not to forget it.

─────────────────────── *WINTER* ───────────────────────

As previously noted, Nature's power and energy are to be found deep inside the earth in wintertime. The depth and intensity of the Winter personality have an entirely different quality from the same characteristics in Autumn. Winter is firmly grounded, and essentially internally motivated. One of the most obvious identifying characteristics of a person linked to Winter is his inability to suffer fools – at all, never mind gladly. When people hear this, particularly if they themselves are linked to Autumn, they often recognize it as typical of themselves. The key difference with Winter, however, is that they will not waste time or energy trying to convert foolishness; they will simply move on, possibly indulging themselves with a sarcastic put-down. Passionate Autumn will stop and explain, fifty different ways, if that is what it takes, and try to set the world to rights.

Another cause for misinterpretation is the oft quoted dramatic quality of Winter; excitable people – drama queens (and kings) – relate to that, but Winter has no need to create a drama, it is inherent. When a Winter personality walks into the room, everyone is aware of his or her arrival, without the need for a word. Winter never over-accessorizes. Many Winter women reject bright colours, living and dying in unadorned black (which they can wear well, with or without make-up, at any time of the day or night), with only occasional touches of white, or possibly royal blue or rich red, and one spectacular piece of fine jewellery; diamonds are only ever completely at home on the Winter woman. The organization of their wardrobes is usually entirely within their perfectionistic control and very simple; they are quite aware of the power they draw and express through minimalism. This concept is supported by sharp angles – geometric prints – shiny but luxuriant fabrics such as heavy white satin or black pure silk velvet; mirrors, glass and chrome. Perfume is likely to be sophisticated, and possibly heavy.

A sense of space is critical for a Winter personality, and I always recommend that any Winter-linked person make every effort to ensure at least thirty minutes a day of silence – meditation is a good way to meet this fundamental need. HRH The Duke of Edinburgh and Elvis Presley represent two very different aspects of the Winter pattern.

Another expression of the seasonal personalities can often be seen in people's hair: Spring suits curls, and if, due to individual variation, they are born with straight hair, they will suit a perm. Summer hair is typically fine, and may contain a soft wave or hint of curl, which is unlikely to suit being cut too short. The 'crowning glory' referred to in the Bible was describing the archetypal Autumn; like everything else about the pattern, Autumn hair will be abundant, plenty of it, whether straight or curly, long or short. Winter hair will be either sleek or extremely curly (no half measures), and

FOREST AUTUMN: IT IS A COMMON MISCONCEPTION THAT BLACK PEOPLE ARE USUALLY WINTER, BUT THESE WINTER COLOURS ARE VERY HARSH FOR JENNIFER.

WOW!

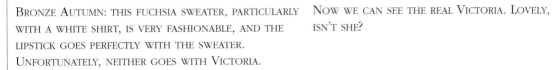

BRONZE AUTUMN: THIS FUCHSIA SWEATER, PARTICULARLY WITH A WHITE SHIRT, IS VERY FASHIONABLE, AND THE LIPSTICK GOES PERFECTLY WITH THE SWEATER. UNFORTUNATELY, NEITHER GOES WITH VICTORIA.

NOW WE CAN SEE THE REAL VICTORIA. LOVELY, ISN'T SHE?

lend itself to dramatic cuts, whether geometric, reminiscent of Quant and Sassoon in the 1960s, short and sharp, or long and sensuous.

Voices, too, can provide clues. The typical Spring personality will have a light, clear voice, and tinkling laugh; Summer expresses itself in soft tones, Autumn's voice is rich and often husky, while Winter's clipped precision is likely to be expressed in cut glass tones, regardless of the origins.

SUBORDINATE INFLUENCES

Having put considerable energy into absorbing these insights, into learning and understanding the typical characteristics, and recognizing the patterns, I am afraid you must be prepared for the disappointment of rarely encountering an absolute archetype; it is disappointing not to see them everywhere. As I have said, although each of us falls absolutely into one of the patterns, we are all tempered by subordinate influences of another pattern. So, for example, the influence of Spring could make the expressions of a basically autumnal pattern lighter, both visually and in the personality, than the archetype. One could be quite attracted to Spring perfumes, plenty of light, blond wood and lots of plants growing in the home, but still be linked absolutely to Autumn.

Or there could be a touch of Summer. Sometimes, when a man with soft colouring and a quiet personality unexpectedly displays a flash of temper and rebels, he, and everyone around him, is amazed. If he understands that he is a Mellow Autumn – one whose essence is rich, fiery Autumn, but whose variations are influenced by cool gentle Summer to the point of practically obscuring the real person underneath – he will wear colours which, whilst still soft and gentle, are warm and supportive, and he will not be drained and repressed by the negative effects of sending out conflicting signals.

Nevertheless, the operative word is subordinate, and the bedrock of a character derives absolutely from one pattern. The fact that an autumnal person is light, and may have some characteristics of Spring or Summer (or even both), is entirely relative. In practical terms, it means that he or she is most supported by colours, fabrics and styles which are at the softer, lighter end of the Autumn palette. It does not mean wearing Spring or Summer colours will work: if one were to cross the borderline and wear those tones, they would not work at all. There seems to be a lot of confusion about this, but it is really very simple – the basic pattern is absolute.

Whilst it is important to understand the concept of subordinates with absolute clarity, it is not necessary to become weighed down with its complexities. Provided a person only ever wears colours which relate to his or her own seasonal pattern, he or she will derive all the benefits – and each individual will instinctively tailor his approach to accommodate quirks. It is however necessary to be aware of the existence of the principle of subordinate influences so that you will not be confused when trying to identify yourself. Very often, we present a face to the public which is a subordinate aspect of ourselves.

CLASSIC WINTER: IN THEORY THIS TAN JACKET SHOULD MAKE ALISON LOOK MORE BUSINESSLIKE — IN FACT IT JUST MAKES HER LOOK UNCOMFORTABLE.

THE ELEGANT SIMPLICITY OF BLACK SILK, WITH A TOUCH OF SILVER JEWELLERY, IS ALL SHE NEEDS TO EXPRESS HER STRENGTH.

SOPHISTICATED WINTER. FRANZ'S EYES ARE QUITE A WARM BROWN, SO A WARM BURGUNDY JACKET SEEMED LIKE A GOOD IDEA. IN FACT IT LOOKS VERY HARSH.

ONLY A WINTER PERSONALITY CAN SUSTAIN A BLACK POLO-NECK SWEATER.

Among the Northern California colourists, led by Suzanne Caygill, several 'types' within each season have been identified and named. In my early years of working there my teacher and I named many more. The following examples are not absolutes, by no means cast in stone, but they may help to cast more light on the subject:

SPRING CAN BE:

Floral Bouquet Winter subordinate. Able to wear a broad spectrum of colours. Brown hair.

Floral A Summer subordinate influence and pink tones in the skin.

Bandbox Winter subordinate with distinct crispness in both personality and appearance.

Golden Strong Autumn subordinate – often blonde hair and unexpectedly husky voice.

Wild Flower Strong Summer subordinate, and very delicate colouring. Blue eyes.

Early Spring Autumn subordinate, but also delicate – particularly good in soft, clear yellows.

Sunny Spring Pure Spring, no subordinate influence, very outgoing personality.

Buoyant Summer subordinate influence, gently sparkling personality.

Radiant Winter subordinate influence. Blonde. Lively personality.

Vital Dark hair and fair skin – often mistaken for Winter, so strong is the subordinate influence.

Saucy Eternally youthful personality, with clarity in both colour and personality coming from the Winter subordinate.

Blithe Summer subordinate influence, an airy quality.

Bubbly Winter subordinate and very effervescent character.

SUMMER CAN BE:

Iridescent The only red-haired Summer. Pink cast to the skin, and blue eyes. Spring subordinate.

English Very cool personality and a Winter subordinate.

Rose Garden Spring subordinate influence. Noticeably pink-toned skin.

Royal Winter subordinate influence, rather aloof.

Twilight Pure Summer – no subordinate influence.

MELANIE, WITH HER FAIR HAIR AND BLUE EYES, COULD BE MISTAKEN FOR SPRING OR SUMMER. SHE IS IN FACT A MELLOW AUTUMN AND LOOKS HER BEST IN WARM, GLOWING COLOURS.

Floral Spring subordinate influence, delicate colouring.

Jewel Tone Often mistaken for Winter – usually dark colouring and much stronger personality than is typical.

Heather Autumn subordinate, unusually warm golden lights in the hair, relatively warm personality.

Serene Winter subordinate, a quietly confident personality .

Elegant Very graceful movements and delicate bone structure. Winter subordinate, if any.

Ethereal Spring subordinate influence and rather 'misty' quality.

Platinum Very light colouring – hair often goes white prematurely, but is not ageing. Winter subordinate.

AUTUMN CAN BE:

Spice Golden tones in the eyes and a strong subordinate Spring influence. Bubbly.

Tawny The name relates to the eye colour – the personality is distinctly offbeat. Spring subordinate.

Bronze Hair the exact colour of bronze, and eyes dark brown – deceptively light personality because of the Spring subordinate.

Sunset Glowing personality – no subordinate. Particularly good in golden reds and orange.

Firelight Similar to Sunset, but not as strong – a Winter subordinate tempers the warmth.

Heather Soft colouring and personality, considerable influence of Summer. Warm purples and blue-green heather tones excellent.

Forest Brunette, usually with green or hazel eyes and a quality of containment in the personality. Winter influence.

Bird of Paradise Extremely flamboyant. Spring subordinate influence.

Amber Summer subordinate. Eye or hair colouring like opaque amber. Gentle personality.

Topaz Similar to Amber, but with a Spring subordinate and more sparkle.

Candlelight Summer subordinate influence and cooler, creamy colouring.

Rembrandt Most often mistaken for Winter – strong subordinate. Good in dark colours.

Feline Winter subordinate – moves like a cat, reminiscent of a panther or a leopard.

Chestnut Red hair and blue eyes. Spring subordinate.

Pewter Hair goes grey prematurely. Winter subordinate.

WINTER CAN BE:

Dramatic No subordinate influence and considerable drama in the personality.

Soft Morning Mist Strong subordinate influence of Summer – clear, but softened

Exotic Usually brunette . Autumn subordinate

Glamorous No subordinate.

Sparkling Delicate bone structure and Spring influence.

Fireworks Spring influence – effervescent personality, which positively fizzes.

Classic Summer subordinate – very cool.

Sophisticated Autumn subordinate – often very iconoclastic.

Regal Summer influence and awe-inspiring personality.

Operatic Autumn subordinate leads to preference for more bright colours than is typical.

There are three blonde Winter types: **Patrician** – Summer subordinate, and impressive bearing; **Champagne** – Autumn subordinate, more warmth in the colouring and personality; **Diamond** – very fair colouring and crystal clarity in both looks and personality; Spring subordinate.

Most of these names are obviously more appropriate for women – men tend not to delve that far into their colour patterns; once they establish the predominant seasonal link, they are more interested to pursue understanding of spectral colour psychology, so we have not specifically named male types. Some, such as the aforementioned Mellow Autumn, can obviously be applied to all.

Like every complex subject, the concept of colour psychology is – as previously mentioned – fraught with paradox. Information received through the right brain is invariably absolutely reliable, but the challenge lies in learning to recognize when it is the right brain that is functioning and when it is a Freudian, unconscious expression of something in a dark recess of the mind.

It may be, for example, that a person reacts against a colour which would normally be a supportive influence, and looks wonderful, but he can't see it because its conscious or unconscious associations with something uncomfortable in that individual's past are negating the positive perceptions – like, for example, the colour of a hated school uniform, or a particular tone which a neurotic parent insisted upon imposing. If this is the case, it is never advisable to force the issue, and try to 'get used' to wearing it, until and unless you feel ready to do so. Do not let anyone, no matter how well-meaning or 'professional', persuade you otherwise. We shall examine examples of that later.

Conversely, one might be attracted to a colour which represents something to which one aspires – however unrealistically. Learn the difference between admiration for something or someone and identification with it or him/her.

As we explore the deeper complexities of colour psychology, we sometimes appear to break the rules, but it is not really so; like any other profound concept, the more we understand it the less hard and fast become the rules. One rule I have found it advisable never to break, however, is:

> If you are trying to see visually what colours are most positively linked to you, do not attempt to compare the harmony of alternatives simultaneously.

One sometimes sees photographs of subjects, with, say, Spring colours draped across one shoulder and Summer colours across the other. It is impossible under these circumstances to see either of the alternatives clearly. The eye does not register only that which is in direct central focus; it takes in the whole picture, including the peripheral field of vision. A diluted and confused story is the inevitable result. Alternatives must always be put out of sight. This is a very common error in graphic design too – designers will compare tiny chips of colour all at once, instead of contemplating the alternatives one at a time in order to absorb the full effect.

CHAPTER SEVEN

Colours in Your World

Until recently in human history, most people lived their lives more or less in the part of the world where they were born, and we were all designed accordingly. Different cultures across the world have very specific characteristics, and they are expressed in the architecture, traditional fashion and art of a region, as well as in the temperament of its people. This is not to say that every person in a particular region of the world is exactly the same as every other, obviously; it is noticeable, however, that certain fundamental attitudes and perspectives are typical – we recognize 'Inscrutable Orientals' 'Fiery Latins' 'Gallic charm'.

Having said that, in today's global village your ethnic origin does not necessarily determine which pattern you relate to. Some experts believe that it is possible for a black person to be Spring-related, but I have never met anyone in this category. I have reservations about it, since light and lightness are such key aspects of Spring; I find it difficult to reconcile the typical characteristics of Spring with dark skin and depth of colouring. However, I do not dismiss the possibility completely, and it has been my experience that, with this one exception, all the four groups can be found in all ethnic types.

We are so accustomed to assessing what colours suit us on the basis of extremely superficial criteria, such as 'blondes look good in blue'; 'redheads shouldn't wear red', that it comes as quite a shock to discover that it is far from unusual for a blue-eyed blonde white person and an Afro-Caribbean black person to belong to the same pattern (often Autumn) and therefore to look and feel good in the same kind of colours.

Of course there are millions of colours in each group, so the chances are that each of these two people will instinctively gravitate towards a different part of the palette – but the truth is their palette is the same and they have more in common with each other than they would have with one of their own ethnic origin who fell into a different season. (Neither of them, if they are Autumn, will look good in black.) This is the reason why this book avoids too much visual description, and emphasizes instead the psychological traits of the four types. The visual enhancement of wearing colours from your own palette is a by-product.

PATTERNS AROUND THE GLOBE

Winter-linked personalities predominate in the Orient and Asia, and in certain parts of the Middle East, where extreme climatic conditions prevail. We tend to think of Oriental people as demonstrably unsentimental and efficient (they are not unfeeling – it is simply that they do not allow sentiment to divert them from their objectives). The whole huge country of China, for example, with its hundreds of millions of people, remains largely contained and something of a mystery; it never seems to have been seized with the wish to open itself out to the rest of the world. We also see evidence everywhere of the material aspiration and hard-working ambition of Asian people.

Southern European and African personalities are rich, extroverted and often very fiery. The colours of the Kalahari Desert, the dramatic beauty of the Black Forest, Tuscany or Provence, England's 'green and pleasant land' – all echo the autumnal patterns. Further north, in Scandinavia, we find a predominance of Spring-linked people. (Remember, one of the most crucial considerations for a Spring-linked personality is light; if you come from the Land of the Midnight Sun it is logical for your appreciation of light to be highly developed.)

There is no part of the world where Summer predominates, but I am advised that there does seem to be a higher than average percentage of them in Norway, for some reason. If that is so, it is interesting when we consider Norway's role in world events. At the time of writing, we are particularly aware that Norway's politicians were instrumental in soothing the troubled Middle East and bringing warring factions together. At the same time, they prefer to remain aloof from the European Union.

Any international business person will confirm the noticeable characteristics of different cultures. I am told, for example, that the first thing an English person is likely to notice, when entering a meeting or conference room in Sweden, is the light, bright (Spring) colours of the men's ties.

Further thought about this brings us again to a recognition of the supreme logic of it all. Nature compensates for the features of the natural environment in the typical characteristics of the indigenous population. So, in hot countries, or parts of the world where extreme climatic conditions prevail, and the light is strong and bright, the people have strong, intense personalities and relatively dark colouring (predominantly Winter and Autumn). These people instinctively wear vivid colours (or the intense total absorption of black). Their skin is protected from the intense sunlight by the presence of much higher levels of melanin than that of the population in more northerly parts, where the need is to maximize the light and encourage the absorption of essential vitamin D. In Britain, the conditions are temperate, without extremes, but we are predominantly inclined to need and respond to warmth and light (Spring and Autumn).

The indigenous populations of the 'New World' countries – Maoris, Native Americans and Australian Aborigines – seem to be predominantly autumnal in their dark, warm colouring and these colours are again echoed in the landscapes, but the settlers came to these countries from all over the world, so there is much more diversity in their modern populations, and no particular seasonal orientation seems to predominate.

RECOGNIZING YOUR OWN PATTERN

It is uplifting and enlightening to study and recognize the characteristics of other cultures, and – as artists and fashion designers often do – use them as inspiration for our own creative expression. We are all part of the human family, and on one level we are all the same. But we must recognize and celebrate the differences – without falling into the trap of trying to adopt inappropriate expressions for ourselves. There is a difference between admiration, as in: 'Oh! Those are wonderful colours!' and personal identification, as in: 'Oh! Those are my kind of colours!' In the highest forms of personal expression it is vital to recognize that difference. Once we find out what our true nature is, we should try not to lose sight of it.

Although I am obviously passionate about colour, nevertheless I do not recommend that anyone should try and achieve a fully co-ordinated life overnight. There are literally millions of shades, tones and tints available to us, and the clothes we have in our wardrobe, the colours in our homes, are all for better or worse expressing something which is or has been a part of us – even if what we have been trying to express amounts almost to total rejection of our whole selves. The process of bringing harmony into one's life should not be rushed, nor should it be inflexible.

When I first began to apply these principles to myself, I did not allow time for a gradual process, but invested in discarding in one go all garments which were not supportive, and buying new. The disadvantage of doing that was that it was painful – rather like using willpower to diet, instead of genuinely working through the attitudes at the heart of the problem. Giving away an elegant black dress which was imbued with visions of myself as the ultimate cool glamour puss (and actually did constitute some protection, as black provides a kind of security) took will power, which I was only able to apply because it was obviously unacceptable not to practise what I was about to start preaching. It sets up a certain amount of psychological resistance, which is never a good idea.

However, the reward for completing this process was quite unexpected. I suddenly began to develop real insight into the potential of colour psychology. We do not see ourselves objectively when we look in the mirror – we only see a collection of preconceived perceptions – but every time I opened the wardrobe in the morning and experienced a rather nice lift of spirits at the picture presented by the colours inside, I reminded myself that this was a reflection of the real me. As I became more and more familiar, and indeed happy, with it I began to realize that I was imperceptibly growing more familiar – and much happier – with myself.

Most people do not complete the process of changing their whole wardrobe. Old habits die hard, and until you have done it yourself it is difficult to believe that a pair of black shoes is not essential. My equivalent of black quickly became dark olive green, or rich dark chocolate brown. Any step in the direction of harmonizing one's life is a step in the right direction, but I find it sad that more people never give themselves the opportunity to enjoy that wonderful, inexplicable extra dimension that can so enhance our lives. People who take the concept on board to that degree almost invariably make big changes in life, as they learn to understand themselves better, and sooner or later they usually apply for training in colour science. They can see the effects, and they want to know for themselves the deeper joys. If people are simply applying on the basis of establishing a lucrative career for themselves, I would not encourage them. Those who want to study the subject for its own sake, out of a love of colour, or of mankind, are far more likely to be open to it and derive the most benefits.

In the early years, I did not consciously draw very much on my training in Freudian psychology, but there were a number of unexpected incidents which began to alert me to the possibilities. They also demonstrated the point made earlier about how response to a potentially very positive colour can be unexpectedly negative, if the associations with whatever it is that that colour represents are painful.

One day a very nice woman came to see me. She was clearly linked to the Autumn pattern, extremely attractive, and some of the strong Autumn golds and dramatic peacock blues looked glorious on her. Then we tried a rich, rosy brick colour, which was the best yet – quite sensational. Before I had time to comment, she turned away from the mirror.

'I don't like that colour!'

Her mood had changed completely.

'What do you associate it with?' I asked gently, aware that we had struck a raw nerve.

'I don't know – I just hate everything about it!'

Such was the nature of the rapport that we had established, that I felt able to say,

'You know, that particular colour relates to the body, and physical considerations. Is there something in that area of your life that you would like to talk about?'

To my surprise, she dissolved into heart-rending sobs. It emerged that she had never had much confidence in her own sexuality and was at the time going through a major crisis, as her husband had been having an affair. She had booked the consultation just to give herself a bit of a boost, but we opened up some very important areas for her. This particular colour exactly expressed her sexuality, and she could not deal with it. We talked the whole thing through, and she allowed herself, for the first time, the blessed relief of tears.

I suggested that she might like to come back again and talk more, and we used colours to help her through the crisis, over a period of several weeks.

Although this incident had given me considerable food for thought, it was only when a second similar insight emerged during a consultation that I decided to go further into the implications of colour psychology in this context. This time, I was working with a beautiful Spring lady, a former actress. She had very blue eyes, and blue is often a keynote hue for a Spring-linked person, but I noticed that she had none of this colour, neither in her wardrobe nor in the decor of her house, which we were also working on. When I asked her about this, she said that she had not noticed, but now that I mentioned it, she was not particularly attracted to blue. On closer questioning it emerged that she had liked blue very much as a small child. I asked,

'How did you do at school? Did you achieve many "O'" levels or "A" levels? University?'

'Oh I was a complete dunce!' she replied: 'I got hardly any GCEs.'

By this time, we had been working together for a while, and I knew that she was by no means stupid. She was a highly intelligent, predominantly right-brained woman. Indeed, she was very gifted and had starred in a serious play in London's West End when she was only twenty-one years old, so she could hardly be deemed a dunce. I suggested to her that she had unconsciously rejected blue as having no part to play in her life, and that looking at it was a reminder of her perceived inadequacies. As I explained in Chapter Two, the colour blue evokes and expresses intellectual activity, but the reaction is usually unconscious, so most people do not realize it.

This lady was astounded at the accuracy of the observation, and admitted that she was sensitive about academic achievement, and still saw herself as something of a dimwit. We introduced a few touches of blue into her decor, to enable her to come to terms with it gradually. She was surprised at her own resistance to it at first, but eventually she began to like the colour – which she could see contributed very positively to the colour scheme we were creating – and as she came to terms with blue she began to like herself better and rebuild confidence in her intellectual ability. When she bought herself a bright blue sweater, it was a great step forward for her.

I have little patience with the 'quick fix' approach to psychological healing. It seems to me that pain or trauma which has been there, building and reinforcing itself for twenty, thirty, who knows how many years, is not going to be identified, acknowledged and healed overnight. I am therefore careful about making unrealistic claims for the efficacy of colour psychology in healing disturbed lives. I am prepared to say, however, that it has a part to play and, as a purely diagnostic tool, it can cut through months or even years of therapeutic searching, and quickly identify troubled areas of the psyche with absolute accuracy.

Whilst psychology is a very young science – it was only acknowledged in its own right and given a name little more than a hundred years ago – the science of colour is as old as time. We have always instinctively recognized its powerful influence and made effective use of its symbolism.

CHAPTER EIGHT

Is Your Freudian Slip Showing?

People often ask if our colour patterns change as we get older. They do not – your colour pattern is genetic, and as unchanging and unique as your fingerprint. However, although the pattern is constant, our personalities and our physical colouring do tend to tone down with maturity. If, like Picasso, you go through a 'blue period', this is an indication of a specific psychological mode, which you may be in for several years. You will come through it much more positively if you ensure that the blues you choose are in the right tonal family for you. Children tend to prefer the stronger, brighter end of their spectrum. Often when a woman finds that there are colours she used to wear which she simply cannot get away with now that she is older, she assumes that her colouring has changed. The truth is they were never good colours for her. Harmonious colours make us look and feel younger, healthier and less tired – but when we are young, we can get away with negative colours because we *are* younger, healthier and less tired! If a colour is right for you, you can wear it at any time of the day or night, with or without make-up, from the day you are born to the day you die. You may gravitate towards different parts of your personal spectrum as you go through different stages of your life, but your spectrum itself does not alter.

There is another aspect to all of this which I have not yet mentioned: within each individual's palette, there are five specific colours which work particularly effectively for that person, in that they echo and support the five basic psychological modes. These are:

1. Your Power Colour – the one which will encourage people to take you seriously. No one will 'pat you on the head' when you are dressed in it.

2. Your Romantic Colour – the colour which will emphasize your sexuality.

3. Your Focal Colour. Stress can derive from your being extremely fraught and needing to be soothed. This is the ideal colour to help you in that situation.

4. Your Dramatic Colour. Another form of stress comes from the lack of energy associated with depression. This colour will lift your spirits and create a positive visual impact on others.

5. Your Contrast Colour. This is the colour which captures the essence of your entire personality. It will not necessarily give you any extra energy but, if you are already feeling good, it will create the maximum impact, projecting the full force of your personality.

I cannot offer general advice on how to establish what these five colours are in your case – it is such an individual matter. Although there is a simple formula to help, it really only points in the general direction of where in the palette to start looking; essentially, finding the precise colour is a matter of instinctive recognition. This is powerful stuff and I have never told anyone what the formula is (although I will confirm it for anyone who figures it out for themselves). I suggest, however, that, as you become more attuned to your own self and your own palette, you focus attention on this question. It is the personal application of colour psychology at its very best.

There is no such thing as a good colour or a bad colour; it is all relative. Tomato red may be an overstatement on one person, quite stunning on another. Now that we have the benefit of deeper insights into people's colour patterns, it is time to examine what we unconsciously reveal about ourselves with our colour choices.

In Chapter Two we learned that the seven spectral hues relate to different physiological functions, and that there are four psychological primary colours – red, blue, green and yellow, relating respectively to the body, the mind, balance and the ego.

People imagine that a colour psychologist must conduct an in-depth contemplation of mood and required behaviour before getting dressed every morning. The truth is at the same time much simpler than that and much more complicated. There are practical questions pertaining to the state of the laundry – what is clean (and preferably ironed)? – and your current weight – what can you get into? There is the weather to be considered, and the diary. In practice, most of us, myself included, reach automatically for the outfit that feels right, without much thought.

The time for in-depth contemplation is not first thing in the morning, under duress, but much earlier, in the shop, before buying any clothes. Thus, if you have the right clothes in your wardrobe, whatever colours you wear will always fulfil the positive role required of them, without your needing to think about it. I rarely give it any conscious thought, but sometimes the significance of the colour I have chosen to wear registers with me in the middle of a meeting and I smile to myself at the recognition of what my unconscious expectations of this meeting, or possibly this whole day, were.

RED

If, for example, you have gone forth in the morning wearing a bright red dress, or tie, or jacket, this means one of several alternatives: you may be feeling slightly below par on a physical level and know that red will give you a boost; conversely you may be full of energy and happy for the world to know it; you may wish to assert yourself, knowing that red makes the maximum visual impact; possibly there is a wish to play down femininity (whichever gender you are). You may even literally be preparing to go into battle!

If you only possess reds which are in tune with you, one or all of these results will derive from wearing red. If you have completely the wrong shade of it on, it will strain you physically; it communicates either defiance or aggression, and makes everyone around you feel less than comfortable; it amounts to an obvious attempt to make a strong statement which does not ring true.

BLUE

Blue is said to be the world's favourite colour – i.e. it is the favourite colour of more adults who have been asked than any other. Perhaps we unconsciously recognize the need for sweet reason and calm, logical thought in this mad world we live in? When people wear blue it encourages them to centre themselves and concentrate on work requiring mental effort. Lighter tones indicate a reflective mood and a wish for gentleness; the darker the blue the more efficient and authoritative. Interestingly, this association has become so entrenched in our conscious awareness that the reassuring strength and authority of navy blue assert themselves regardless of the wearer. This explains its widespread use and success in the design of uniforms. People respond to the uniform, rather than to the person. In the case of police officers, firefighters, airline pilots and the like, this is essential.

The negative properties of blue derive from its coolness. The wrong kind of blue can be very aloof and unfriendly – perhaps too businesslike. It is essentially a bland, calming colour and can be draining. Many people choose to hide behind dark navy; Autumn women in particular often adopt navy blue as the corner-stone of their working wardrobe. In some respects, this is entirely appropriate, and it does put out the fire. The problem is that the fire is an essential part of that person's make-up, and really should not be extinguished completely. Far better that it should just be banked down by the right shade of dark blue – deep teal, or petrel. For different reasons, brown can achieve a similar positive result, insofar as it is inherently a serious colour and works well for any Autumn woman who wants to be taken seriously. Working women, keen to assert themselves in what they see as a male-dominated world, often dismiss this alternative and think that brown will make them look dreary – but a rich, warm brown is very powerful on a richly dramatic person with warm colouring; far more so than the deadening effect of cold navy.

People imagine that dress codes determine colours much more rigidly than they actually do. Darker colours add weight and gravitas; it would still be inappropriate to wear frothy, light colours at work if you wished to be perceived as professional and businesslike, but it is not necessary to limit oneself to dark grey or navy any more. I am delighted to see so many men being much more adventurous in the colours of their business suits, now that old restrictions about colours for the country never coming into the city have been removed. These days it is as it should be – colours for the person.

The next stage, hopefully, is when men realize that white shirts and black shoes belong to the old regime of dark grey and navy. White shirts do not look right with any other colour of jacket, except for a black dinner jacket (or tails).

NATURE HOLDS THE KEY TO SO MUCH OF OUR APPRECIATION OF COLOUR. ALTHOUGH WE CAN NEVER RECREATE HER MATCHLESS HARMONIES, WE CAN LEARN FROM THEM. GREEN, FOR EXAMPLE, IS THE COLOUR OF PERFECT BALANCE.

GREEN

If you reach for green in the morning, you are probably looking forward to a fairly relaxed day, different in quality from the soothing tranquillity

imposed by blue. You are at peace with yourself and the world, and feeling positively balanced. Remember that green strikes the eye at the point requiring no adjustment, and is therefore restful; it relates to love in the universal sense. Obviously there are bright greens to be seen everywhere, and although they are focusing on the same area of the psyche, they do so in a different way from the mid-tone olive or sage greens, moss or forest. An intense colour – whatever the hue – contains more energy and is by definition less restful. Nevertheless, green is about balance, and that is the key factor being expressed when someone wears it. Bright green may simply express a delicious sense of harmony with the world, which you wish to state in unequivocal terms. A bright-eyed Spring person in vivid emerald green is a joy to behold.

Again, however, it is possible to get it very wrong. That same bright-eyed Spring, perhaps inspired by the earthy autumnal greens of environmentally aware, eco-friendly political correctness, can drag him or herself down to bland dreariness by the suppression brought about by green's negative face.

Green is often considered unlucky, and some people become quite irrational in their attitudes towards it, refusing to have any green garment or object in their lives. There are two possible reasons for this. One is a phenomenon known as the Green Flash, whereby when the dawn air is exceptionally clear, the atmospheric particles catch the light in such a way as to send a momentary flash of green across the sky. This occurred the morning that the volcano Krakatoa erupted in Indonesia in 1883. It is hardly surprising, therefore, that people in that part of the world see green as a portent of disaster. The other association is with decay and disease; on the battlefield of the Crimea in the 1850s a soldier who had been shot in the leg stood a reasonable chance of retaining the injured limb – unless (or until) it turned green, which indicated gangrene and a very poor chance of recovery.

It is unfortunate that green has acquired these associations, as it is the most effective healing colour. As we have seen, it is the colour of balance and universal love. It is far more supportive, for instance, in time of bereavement than the absolute oppression of black, or excessive introversion of deep purple. City-dwellers almost invariably feel refreshed and restored by spending time in the greenery of the country – or even an hour in the park.

YELLOW

Yellow is a colour which people are often slightly nervous of wearing. It is essentially light and highly visible. What perhaps most of us do not realize is that the caution is quite appropriate, but for entirely different reasons – because yellow focuses on the ego, optimism and self-esteem. It stimulates and takes the mind outward and forward. Yellow is the perceived colour of sunlight and lifts our spirits, but too much of it, or the wrong yellow, presents considerable strain and can indicate that self-esteem is not at its

THIS DELICATE SHADE OF
PEACH HAS SENSUAL
ASSOCIATIONS, BUT IS
SOOTHING AND
COMFORTING. A
STRONGER VERSION OF
THE SAME COLOUR
WOULD BE FIERY AND
PASSIONATE.

highest and a rather desperate attempt is being made to disguise the fact. It should be chosen with great caution by people coming into contact with emotionally fragile people – Samaritans, for instance, or those working in psychiatric hospitals.

In Imperial China, yellow was considered a sacred colour. Only the Emperor was allowed to wear it – an ego trip if ever there was one!
These four primary colours create the context. The fun does not really start until we look at the way we mix them. Around the basic 'red' description lie literally millions of shades, tones and tints. In practice, most colours are a mixture, and will therefore evoke a mixture of emotions. So burgundy, pinks, peaches, maroon, browns – all these colours derive from red and are fundamentally physical, but are modified, emphasized or even toned down completely, by the other colours combining with the basic red to produce the predominant shade being worn. Then the secondary shades introduce their own combination of properties into the mix.

The 'blue' arena encompasses a wide range too, from pure sky blue through turquoises, the aquamarine tones of the sea, the periwinkle and lavender blues taking us towards violet, to the velvet depths of the night sky. They are all related to the intellect and reflection.

Yellow – whether it is pure daffodil or deep butter, lemon or banana, whether it has black added and is on the borders of olive green, or white added and could be more accurately described as cream – expresses the ego and self-esteem, creativity and optimism. As previously mentioned, yellow is at the core of Spring and Autumn palettes, being the basic expression of light and extroversion, so there are many variations of yellow in those palettes. Summer and Winter contain very few.

VIOLET

The other important colour which takes us to a specific part of the human psyche is violet. This colour relates to the higher mind and the spirit, and is of course every bit as important as the other four (probably more so, but it has not been particularly identified as a psychological primary by traditional colour scientists). In the East the seventh chakra – the highest level of spiritual evolution – relates to the pineal gland, sometimes known as the site of the soul; pure white, the sum of all colours, is sometimes ascribed to it, but more often it is violet.

Violet is introvertive and usually indicates that the wearer prefers to be left alone, in peaceful contemplation. It provides a kind of barrier which will protect from insensitive or thoughtless demands. The right tone, on the right person, can stop people dead in their tracks – but do be sure you have the right tone, as it will turn you in upon yourself to an unhealthy degree if you are not careful. The Summer palette contains many variations of short wave-length violet in its lighter values – cool mauves – and one of Winter's most supportive colours is the classic deep purple. The extrovert Spring and Autumn do have their own versions of violet, of course, but not so many, and it does not play such a major part in their personal palettes.

PINK

Pink is the purest expression of femininity. (Remember, every single one of us contains elements of both masculinity and femininity, which it is healthy to express from time to time.) A tint of red, pink is physically soothing and represents the feminine principle, focusing on nurturing and survival of the species (where, as we have seen, masculine red is about basic survival – fight or flight). Pink is quite a sexy colour with its obvious associations with flesh, and its unconscious evocation of the parenting instinct. If you believe the old joke that a man spends the first nine months trying to get out of the womb and the rest of his life trying to get back in, then it is easy to understand the sex appeal of pink. It is important to understand, however, that pink misused – i.e. too much of it, or the wrong tone – is physically weakening. Many people use it in the decor of their bedrooms; this is fine, as it will encourage physical relaxation and sleep, but unless there is balance, in the form of some green or blue, you will not awaken refreshed in the morning.

ORANGE

Orange is sexy too, in a different way. It is associated with physical enjoyment and fiery passion. Secondary survival instincts are evoked by orange – warmth, shelter, food, physical comfort, security. An inappropriate or badly harmonized orange creates a sense of physical deprivation, which is why it was such a poor choice for decor in Britain's job centres during the 1980s. In fashion, the wrong orange always looks cheap – and conversely, the right orange looks richly abundant and very sensual.

GREY

Grey is the only colour which is totally neutral; it has no psychological properties whatever. In practice it can be used as an elegant neutral, but if you wear it with a rich autumnal colour, the chances are it will negate those warm properties and again put the fire out. More often than not grey is a negative influence, indicating lack of confidence; visually it can either drain the life out of the other colours used with it (or of you!) or make them appear harsh and gaudy. Grey will never actively enhance; the best it will do is quietly support. I am sure we all know people who live and die in grey or black – this indicates low self-esteem and lack of confidence, or actual depression. Grey acquired something of a name for itself as an elegant and expensive 'designer' colour in the 1980s, particularly in interior design, but there was a very specific and contemporary reason for that, as we shall see in Chapter Nineteen. Its value did not carry forward into the 1990s.

BLACK

There are more misconceptions about black than about all other colours put together, and it probably deserves a whole chapter to itself. Most people think it is sophisticated and glamorous, and in a sense this is true. Black is one of the key colours of the Winter palette, and is imbued with all those elegant characteristics of Winter – but only when worn by a Winter-linked personality. Worn by a person of a different nature, it has different properties. Black absorbs all the wavelengths of light, and therefore represents total absorption, absence of light. Some consideration of the implications of both of those concepts will show you what its psychological properties are: absence of light is darkness – and many people are afraid of the dark; black is menacing. It is a heavy colour – only slimming on a person who is already slim – and when you find yourself confronted by an already large person, dressed all in black and therefore appearing even bigger and heavier than they are, you are more than likely to feel a little nervous. The truth may be quite different, because from the wearer's point of view, total absorption provides barriers, a psychological security blanket; often the biker in his black leather, or the Punks, or Goths, are not particularly menacing in reality. It is possible that the protection that black clothes provide gives them more courage.

People often say that they wear a lot of black because it is 'safe', meaning that it will not clash with anything, nor stand out in a crowd and it is always elegant – what they do not realize is that they are more literally right about the sense of safety than they think. I once did some work with a very famous lady, who asked me why I thought she wore so much black. She was a blue-eyed blonde, Spring-linked, with a strong Winter subordinate. I explained to her about this aspect of black; every time this lady stepped out of her house, she was likely to be assailed on all sides by strangers who felt that, because she was so familiar to them, they had a perfect right to approach her. She was always – every minute of the day –

in the public eye, and the need to protect herself, coupled with her Winter subordinate influence, led her to adopt black very readily. Frankly, she does not look good in it; it does not flatter her face, and she needs extra make-up to wear it at all successfully. She saw that for herself when we were working together.

As for the elegance, there is no doubt that a black garment is likely to be more elegant than a brightly coloured one. The key question you must ask yourself, however, is whether you are more elegant in it. If it is 'wearing' you, rather than you wearing it, and your colouring and personality recede when you put it on, then be aware of exactly what you are doing. You may wish to recede and, as it were, let your dress go to the party. When we go out to a social event, we are often nervous; we do not know whom we shall encounter, how we shall be received, how the whole evening will go. We reach for safe black ('the little black dress') and when we get to the party – any and every party – we find that over 80 per cent of our fellow guests are also wearing black.

I once received a telephone call from the head of fashion at a London college, the day after I had attended a very smart party for over 200 guests. She said she had heard that morning from a past pupil, whom I had met the previous evening, suggesting that we discuss the possibility of my talking to the students about my work. The past pupil had told her that I was the only person (male or female) at the party who was not wearing black in some shape or form.

It is entirely understandable; if you are going to wear red, as I did that evening, or any bright colour, you must accept that you will inevitably stand out to some degree, so you need to feel sure that you have got the colour right. Most people are unsure of the exact colours which work for them, so they stick with black. If you do opt for black, do not complain if you are ignored – even when your outfit is admired. Equally, of course, if you are already rather a spectacular personality, black might be a useful way of toning you down a little.

WHITE

When society's mood changed so dramatically from the glitzy, materialistic 1980s to the 'caring, sharing' 1990s, one or two fashion designers in Britain decreed that the best colour to express this new purity was white. One went so far as to produce his whole Spring collection for 1990 in white only – for men, for women and even with children on the catwalk. It was thought that because white has conscious associations with purity and cleanliness, with virginity, it expressed these values.

These designers had missed the point of white completely. Those long-established associations derive from the purely practical reality that any white object or garment which is less than pristine will immediately show up its grubbiness. In terms of caring and sharing, achieving pure white requires too many chemicals for it to express environmental awareness with any true conviction.

Psychologically, white is demanding and can be very harsh, throwing the full force of the spectrum at you. It is uncompromising, hygienic and clinical, with no fine nuances. Like black it creates barriers, but in a different way from the protective absorption of black – white is total reflection, and throws up a wall: 'touch me not'. It is only worn by people who either do not get themselves dirty, or can afford to change their clothes more often than most, so it is not exactly a friendly, informal sort of colour. It is supremely aspirational – there is nothing quite so impressive as a Winter-linked man, wearing a dark suit and a blinding white shirt. The young doctor instantly becomes impressive when the white coat is donned.

People often wear white in the summertime, thinking that it suits them if they have a tan and sets off the glowing skin to advantage. Unless you have cool tones in your skin, it is unlikely to enhance your tan nearly as effectively as a vivid warm green or bright blue, but if you are young you may get away with it and it is understandable to reach for white, the sum of all colours, when you wish to highlight your sunny mood. The most effective colour for showing off a tan is a strong turquoise (in the correct tone for your type).

Often you will see people – particularly women trying to make a name for themselves in the fashion world – adopting the whole Winter palette of colours and style completely. This is appropriate in terms of the elegance of the clothes, but it does not work in the long run to leave yourself out of the equation. Matching up shirts, jackets, ties, trousers, shoes, bags, scarves, skirts with each other, without ever really considering the wearer beyond a passing, superficial acknowledgement, is quite ludicrous, but it

WE TEND TO THINK THAT WHITE IS ALL ABOUT PURITY, AND IN NATURE WHO COULD ARGUE? BUT IN THE HOME OR IN THE WARDROBE IT CAN BE UNCOMPROMISING AND CLINICAL — USE IT WITH CAUTION.

is so common as to be the norm. You see it everywhere in clothes shops –
'This jacket will go beautifully with my new skirt!' – with no apparent
awareness that it is draining the face. On one level people who buy their
clothes in this way are confident because they are dressed in the height of
fashion, but on another, deeper level they are aware that something is not
quite right; they are not quite at ease with their all-important 'image'. This
is when they will probably decide to 'go blonde' or change their hair
colour or their make-up radically in some way. Thus they distance themselves even further from their own unique style, and lose sight completely
of who they are, in the headlong dash towards conformity with fashion.
Eventually neither they, nor anyone else, can relax and enjoy their true
nature and unique beauty.

If there is one message at the heart of this book it is this: remember, the
most important part of your colour scheme is **you**.

PART THREE

COLOUR IN YOUR HOME

CHAPTER NINE

Reconcilable Differences

In Chapter Five we looked briefly at archetypal interior design for each of the four personality types. It is worth reiterating the point made in that chapter about the likelihood of more accurate self-expression being found in the home than in personal presentation. I often meet people who, for example, wear lots of black or navy and generally present themselves to the world in the Winter pattern, and then, when I visit their home, it is all oatmeal and terracotta! Nevertheless a factor which cannot be ignored is that of conditioning. Interior design ideas are inculcated into us from the very start by the home into which we are born; we usually have little choice in the decor of our surroundings for the first sixteen years or so of life, so we adapt ourselves to it.

This is likely to be particularly true of older readers; previous generations did not argue with parental perceptions of 'good taste', and the conditioning can run deep, but you may be agreeably surprised if you stand back and take an objective look at your ideas. Ask yourself, for example, whether you really *like* the Victorian influence in your drawing room, or is it just conditioned habit; question the assumption that you need fitted carpets or traditionally painted woodwork. Younger people are more assertive of their own taste in their homes, but even here it is worth re-examining your ideas to be certain that they are genuinely your own. It has been said to me in the past, on more than one occasion, 'It is quite strange – I thought I was happy enough with my ideas about interior design, but suddenly I feel so much more at home!'

The obvious question, when considering colour psychology in relation to personality types is: when people of different types are living together, how can the interior design of the home support them all?

Essentially, the home is a microcosm of each individual's whole world and its condition directly reflects the state of mind of all the occupants. So mutual attitudes are probably even more relevant than pure personality. There is an old saying that a man approaches decorating the home with exactly the same attitude as he expresses his love for his wife. So, for example, if he spends plenty of love and care on ensuring that the standard of work is of the very highest, if he feels that nothing is too good for his home, at the same time soliciting and respecting his wife's opinions and keeping disruption to the minimum, the chances are he is very much in love. If, on the other hand, he starts off with great enthusiasm, goes to the local DIY shop to buy everything he needs, pulls the whole place apart and then goes off to the pub, leaving everything in chaos (for weeks, or even months) while he 'thinks about it' and his enthusiasm evaporates – we may safely assume that his attitude toward his wife and home is fraught with ambivalence. These observations apply before we even begin to consider the significance of the colour choices.

In pure colour terms, when someone chooses a colour for the home which is an exact reflection of the predominant characteristic of a partner, they may be unconsciously expressing the wish to defer to that partner in all things. If a woman is totally in love, and thrilled to pieces that she is moving in with the man she loves, it may be very supportive for her to live in an environment which expresses his personality, but in the longer term this would not be healthy, as it indicates excessive dependence. Having said that, I know a married couple who have been together for many years: the husband is a rock musician, who spends long weeks on the road, away from home. For as long as I have known them, their living area – open plan sitting room and dining room – has been painted a rather distinctive shade of pink to which I would not expect him to respond. It is, however, an exact expression of his wife's femininity, and he loves it. He told me that he loves coming home to his family, and that colour makes him feel he is returning to the womb. Every three years or so, he just repaints it, the same colour. It has become something of an institution in their family, and visitors are always soothed by it.

There are two ways of reconciling differences. One is to decide on a fairly neutral approach in the common parts of the house and then allow each family member his or her own space somewhere (a study perhaps, or their own bedroom), with complete freedom to decorate it any way that appeals. The other – in my opinion preferable – is to work out what the groups have in common and build from there.

Any two seasons always have something: Spring and Summer have lightness and delicacy in common; Spring and Autumn are both warm, whilst Spring and Winter share a need for clarity and primary colours. Summer and Autumn have subtlety of tone and high quality in common (for different reasons – Autumn requires solid comfort, while Summer abhors anything cheap and inferior); Summer and Winter are both cool. Autumn shares with Winter the depth and intensity typical of each.

Since it is never advisable to try and combine colours from more than one season, the best basis for compromise derives from other considerations – textures, form, proportion, lines, light and dark and use of space. Let us first be clear about the archetypes.

SPRING

Spring is most supported by crisp, fresh, smooth textures, plenty of light, spherical shapes and delicate lines; you do not need to feel a great sense of space, but you must have light; Spring-linked people, or those with a strong subordinate influence of Spring, are the most susceptible to SAD – Seasonal Affective Disorder; you love big windows, and French doors to a

THIS SEATING AREA, BETWEEN TWO LARGE WINDOWS, IS MAINLY SPRING – ROUND SHAPES, LIGHT, BRIGHT COLOURS AND POT PLANTS. THE BLACK AND WHITE FLOORING AND PATTERNED RUG, HOWEVER, ARE TOO HEAVY. A PLAIN FITTED CARPET IN BLUE OR GREEN WOULD COMPLETE THE MOOD.

garden or terrace. Typically you respond to prints and floral patterns featuring small flowers, not large, and the best paint finish for you is eggshell. It is important to avoid introducing anything heavy or dark, as your spirits will be oppressed by, for example, large, imposing chests, wardrobes, tables and other furniture in the mahogany or dark oak so typical of the late Victorian and Edwardian period. You instinctively prefer the new, but you could be happy with the delicacy of the Regency period, or with antique light pine, ash, burr walnut or very light oak. Cottage style chintz and fresh gingham are good for you. Typical Spring responds to cane and wicker, and the rounded Bergère style of three-piece suite would please you. I once knew a Spring-linked lady who inherited a magnificent medium oak dining suite – a large table with six chairs, two carvers and a sideboard with two pillars supporting the top of it and a mirrored back. I almost wept when she decided to have the whole suite bleached. It was, however, quite successful; these days limed oak is very fashionable, so – typical Spring – she was ahead of her time. The trouble was she got rather carried away with enthusiasm and had to be dissuaded from bleaching everything thereafter.

Spring people like gold leaf and gilded finishes, although the only solid metal you are likely to respond to in the home is brass. You love the sparkle of cut crystal, especially beautifully coloured Venetian glass. If you invite guests to dinner, it will never be an ultra formal occasion, but it will be fun, and the table will be presented with great charm – probably no table-cloth, but mats, china with a floral pattern or a gold motif, sparkling cutlery and glass (Spring especially loves those long-stemmed cut crystal wine goblets which come in sets of six different colours) and one or more small posies of fresh flowers on the table. If you are not quite ready when the first guests arrive you will cheerfully recruit them to wash the lettuce or open the wine; Spring does not stand on ceremony.

Spring has a very strong practical streak and you love a bargain. You are sentimental and must be allowed to display mementoes. A Spring couple of my acquaintance have a glass-fronted display cabinet, which extends almost the length of one wall in their drawing room, containing small dolls which they have been collecting, in their travels, for years.

Your preferred kitchen units would be laminate, in a light colour, rather than solid timber (although, as previously mentioned, you could live with limed oak), and you would be well advised to have a light colour on the floor; dark-coloured flooring drags you down psychologically. Usually, typical Spring is a good housekeeper, as anything which is less than fresh, or somewhat crumpled, disturbs you, so the oft quoted reason for avoiding light-coloured flooring – 'it shows the dirt' – would bother you less than most. In the rest of the house fitted carpets are best for you. You must have flowers in your life. If they are not to be found in the decor, make sure you have plenty of house plants around – ferns are particularly good for you; you are more than likely to have 'green fingers'.

SUMMER

Summer prefers softer, S-shaped curves, delicate fabrics, preferably with a slight sheen, and classic proportions. If you are asked to live in a place with a very low ceiling, it will not matter what colours you use, you will never feel completely comfortable. Marble columns and an impressive curved staircase would be more you; this may be a trifle unrealistic, but nevertheless it would be in your best interests to seek out a home in a period building, built in an age where more attention was paid to proportion, and ceilings are higher. On the floor you might appreciate flawless parquet, with perhaps a delicately tinted Chinese rug. If you have fitted carpet it must be good quality and soft underfoot. You too can respond to prints, but much more subtle patterns, slightly impressionist – perhaps open flowers splashed on the fabric, rather than perky Spring buds. The subtle sheen of satin-finish paintwork appeals.

THE COOL GRACE OF THIS ELEGANT ROOM IS PURE SUMMER, ALTHOUGH THERE IS EVIDENCE OF SOME SPRING IN THE RUCHED CURTAINS AND SLIGHT WARMTH IN THE CREAMY CARPET.

Calm and order will be the keynote in your home. You are a classicist and you would be very happy in a home designed in the style of Nash or Adam, surrounded by elegant antiques. You will lovingly polish fine wood – satinwood, rosewood, mahogany are the best for you – and the beauty of intricate craftsmanship as found, for example, in Sheraton furniture inspires you. You love the graceful curve of cabriole legs. With your exquisitely developed sense of touch, the feel of any fabric is of paramount importance to you, so pure silk, damask or fine lace are very supportive. Like Spring, you respond to flowers, but would probably prefer a vase of roses, or a magnificent display of sweet-smelling summer blooms, to potted plants. You also have an appreciation of fine china and would, therefore, enjoy having floral display in that form. The Spanish house, Lladro, creates porcelain figurines whose graceful, fluid lines and delicate colours are virtually designed especially for you.

Your dinner parties will be an elegant delight. You are more formal than Spring, but not out of any wish to fuss or make an impression – rather because your strong nurturing instinct wants to provide nothing but the very best for your guests, and you will go to endless trouble to attend to every detail. The likelihood is that your table will be laid with a fine table-

cloth, possibly lace, delicately curved glassware and, if budget permits, solid silver. If budget does not permit, your top quality brushed steel cutlery will be elegant. You will have a beautifully arranged floral centrepiece. Your bone china would ideally be pale pink or blue, decorated with a silver motif, or flowers. You prefer oval shapes to round.

Your kitchen, like Spring's, will probably be laminate, with plenty of satin-finish stainless steel to be found. Edges will be curved and you would really like a rounded breakfast bar.

AUTUMN

Autumn must feel that the surroundings are substantial and solid. Preferred textures are grained, slubbed or in some way inherently interesting, like linen, raw silk or tweed, rather than patterns (other than a leaf or Paisley print) printed on a smooth fabric. If your walls are painted – a matt finish is probably best for you – you are likely to texture them in some way first with something like anaglypta wallpaper, or you will be attracted to rag rolling and other interesting effects. (One of the less desirable examples of Autumn can be seen if you rent property in Britain and notice landlords' love of magnolia-painted wood-chip wallpaper.) If you prefer papered walls, you will again be advised not to have them too smooth; I am not recommending flock wallpaper, but perhaps hessian would be a possibility. Shiny paper would not be supportive for you, unless you have a very strong Winter subordinate. Lines are beginning to square off, and, whilst Autumn does not respond to having too many knick knacks on display, creating clutter, a good Capo di Monte or anything bronze would be appreciated – you do not particularly need a sense of space. In fact, in my experience Autumn is often quite unaware of a different kind of clutter, which the rest of the world would probably describe as untidy; your squirrel instincts will cause you to preserve everything, and your home might have books, magazines etc. on every surface, and furniture which you cannot bear to part with taking up a lot of room. The 'absent-minded professor' is more than likely Autumn linked, as he is too lost in his passion for knowledge to notice how the room looks.

Your whole approach to your home is less formal than Summer – almost primitive in fact, in that you love the rough beauty of exposed brick or stone, or the warmth of wood; hand woven rugs and tribal artefacts fascinate you. More than most, you need a fireplace in your living area – not the graceful Adam surround favoured by Summer or Spring; rather red brick or stone, in an inglenook, or a typical Victorian design in solid oak; you could even cope with marble or iron, provided they were old enough to have acquired a warm patina. You appreciate antiquity to the point of worship, and it is a great delight to you to find a neglected Victorian or Edwardian house and restore its original features.

At the time of writing, the autumnal approach to interiors is holding sway, in the 'New York Warehouse' feel of converted old buildings of all kinds, which have been restored to provide ultra chic, open-plan homes with exposed beams and stripped wooden doors, floors, etc. and antique tiles. Stone-flagged floors appeal to you and you respond to Middle Eastern rugs. This kind of decor only works in a building which is rock solid and substantial to start with – it is not a look which could be superimposed on a modern box. If you do find yourself living in the latter, you will probably compensate for that in the solid quality of the furnishing: squashy sofas and big, cosy armchairs near a fireplace of some sort. Although you appreciate the efficiency of built-in units, you are not mad about them aesthetically – you prefer free-standing furniture.

Your dining table, like Spring's, will probably not have a table-cloth on it; it will be solid, either a genuine antique – possibly an old refectory table – or a solid teak modern one, with table mats. You are happy with solid timber of any kind, as long as it is not too light – you would be unlikely to appreciate the blond modern pine which is so popular today. Your ideal centre-piece will be dried flowers, lichen or mosses and you love South American or Mexican heavy glassware. Your table would also carry off very well the rustic designs of pottery which are so fashionable now (and often just as expensive, if not more so, as bone china). You are probably the only type who would respond to bronze or brass cutlery –

but you may prefer solid silver, in spite of its cold colour, because of its substantial heaviness. After dinner, you will be likely to take your guests back to the fireside to have coffee, and talk long into the night.

I need hardly add that your ideal kitchen would have solid oak units, and plenty of copper around, in the pans, bowls, etc. The floor would be stone, red tiles or wood. Terracotta is very much you.

WINTER

Winter needs a sense of space – uncluttered vistas. You love very shiny surfaces, like chrome or glass (mirrors), and clean lines, sharp angles, minimalism; you prefer metal, or something even more distinctive, to wood, and you like leather upholstery. You still prefer traditional high-gloss paintwork, contrasting with matt walls. There is a wallpaper which is perfect for you: it came strongly into vogue in the 1970s, and is known as 'distressed foil'; it literally has the pattern printed on the shiny side of aluminium foil, and is, I understand, very expensive and incredibly difficult to apply. You would be the one to appreciate it and recognize that it is more effective in small doses. Contrast is the essence of your decor. Just as the landscape in the depths of winter contains virtually no colour – sometimes nothing but pure snow white – where the sudden drama of a holly tree, or a robin's breast is heightened, so your ideal surroundings will echo the same concept.

You are not particularly attracted to patterns, preferring solid colour, but you could live with crisp stripes or geometric prints. Fashionable design in the materially aspirational 1980s reflected the Winter pattern in all its glory, with white walls, grey or black carpets, white tiled or marble floors and lots of matt black or crimson. In spite of the heightening awareness of animal rights that began to develop over the same period, leather furniture became all the rage, and huge showrooms featuring nothing but leather opened up everywhere. Although you do not respond instinctively to a grained wood finish – you would prefer Chinese lacquer or glass for cupboards, tables, etc. – you can be reasonably happy with fashionable black ash. Your instinctive sense of drama will always lead you to place everything in exactly the right place to maximize its effect. You love Lalique, and will display it to perfection.

When entertaining, if your large dining-table top is not made of plate glass, it will probably have a blindingly white table-cloth on it, and it will be uncluttered, with plenty of room for all the guests to eat in comfort. There is less likelihood of ornate table decoration than of dramatic presentation of the food itself – a whole salmon, beautifully decorated, a crown of lamb, artistically prepared salads which delight the eye as much as the palate. The china, cutlery and glass, always streamlined, will present distinctive examples of contemporary design excellence (often quite witty).

Your ideal kitchen would be a cross between a space station and a science lab. Black high gloss or white laminate doors, white ceramic tile floor and everything possible in polished stainless steel would inspire you.

THE ART DECO MOOD AND VIRTUALLY ACHROMATIC COLOUR SCHEME IN THIS ROOM IS PURE WINTER.

FINDING YOUR COMMON FACTORS

When two people of different seasons live together, the subordinate influences are the factors which will create the ideal compromise. Let us consider some examples.

A dark-haired Spring man, with a Winter subordinate, is married to a honey blonde Autumn woman, with a Spring subordinate; both have blue eyes. In colour terms they have more in common than may be immediately apparent. Throughout the house they will find agreement in the deeper end of Spring colours, provided they can compromise. The husband would be advised not to insist on imposing his appreciation of a bargain wallpaper he found in the bottom of a 'sale' basket. Unless it was a Colefax and Fowler, Harrods or Liberty's sale, his Autumn wife will not appreciate the bargain; her view is that in a few weeks they will have forgotten the price of the paper, but they might have to live with something cheap and tacky for years: a DIY chain store's rejects she would prefer to do without. For her part, she should gracefully compromise on the heaviness of fabrics, and not insist on linen. Her husband would be constantly irritated by his perception of linen: 'It needs ironing!' Spring really needs fresh crispness. These two have a lot in common: warmth, a liking for natural finishes and timber; it is more than likely that they will share a love of blue, and it may also very well be that the wife's Spring subordinate influence will lead her to prefer more light than is typical of Autumn's needs.

If their lifestyle permitted, each room could be one season or the other, around the Spring/Autumn borderline, and the whole would combine to create an accurate expression of this couple. So if they are both working outside the home, and the husband likes being the chef, the kitchen could be light and bright Spring colours; the wife's personality may dominate the autumnal dining room, where she enjoys being the perfect hostess. Individual attitudes and honest communication will determine whose is the dominant influence in the bedroom and the sitting room they share more or less equally, but there is a wide spectrum of colours, all warm, which hover around this particular borderline. Since both these people have considerable Spring influence in them, a fairly light colour scheme, with plenty of warm blues, would work; it is not necessary for either party to be overtly dominant.

Perhaps a more challenging example might be: a Mellow Autumn man (Summer subordinate) marries a Winter woman, with no subordinate at all. Both are brunette, although her colouring is darker than his; his eyes are blue, hers are brown. What do they have in common? He likes warm colours, she prefers cold. Well, they are both hedonists, who would eschew anything cheap or flimsy, and they both contain depth and intensity in their personalities and are therefore quite happy to live with depth and intensity in the colours around them. He, having a very strong Summer subordinate, is at the cool end of the Autumn palette, so he would not insist on lots of fiery colours, but could live with borderline greeny-blues.

That borderline around the jade greens and peacock blues contains a myriad of those tones, in both seasons. They probably both like purples, too. She would opt for white walls, which he would find a strain, but as long as she did not go the whole hog, and want black carpeting and lots of chrome and glass everywhere, he could soften the impact of the white with plenty of pictures on the walls, and possibly a beautiful polished light ash or oak floor. Red is a colour which could feature, as both Autumn and Winter respond to its strength. Provided the place is uncluttered, without being stark, these two should be able to harmonize perfectly, given some thought and the right attitude.

More important than thought is communication. When a couple decide to redecorate, how often do they sit down together at the outset, and really thrash out what they envisage? Very rarely, in my experience. The issues should be clarified, and preferably written down, before anyone goes near a shop. Assuming you completed the questionnaire in Part One, and have an idea of your seasons, ask each other the following questions:

1. What colour do you want this room to be, predominantly?

2. What secondary colour?

3. Where do you want the interest – in a patterned wallpaper? patterned curtains? patterned upholstery? no patterns, but interest deriving from different textures?

4. Is this a room which needs to have a peaceful atmosphere, or a stimulating one?

5. What is your attitude toward the predominant activity that goes on in this room? Is it hard work for you or a delight (the kitchen and the study are two examples of rooms towards which different people might have different attitudes)?

Professional designers put in many hours of this kind of enquiry and analysis before they ever attempt to choose colours or finishes. You will be unlikely to find them wandering around the paint department, looking 'to see what there is'. These days, paint can be mixed to your precise requirements, and ranges of wallpapers and fabrics are so vast that it really pays dividends to have a clear idea of what you want before you go, otherwise it can be overwhelming. Dispiritedly trailing around the stores looking for inspiration is demoralizing, and unlikely to result in the ideal room for you.

In the following chapters, we shall examine the implications of colour choices in various parts of the house, but it is perhaps worth rereading Chapter Eight, so that if your partner is determined to have, let us say, green predominating in the bedroom, and you hate green, you will be able to recognize that he or she is not just being difficult, but is expressing a need for more balance. Why? What is the problem? There may be something underlying this battle which needs to be brought to the surface. And anyway, why do you hate green? Could the two of you compromise with a turquoise? You will be amazed to discover what emerges about you both in the course of this analysis.

Remember, too, the crucial issue of balance. The most effective – and most supportive – colour schemes are those which contain a balance of wavelengths. You may feel that you want an all pink bedroom, but, as previously explained, that would be entirely physical, and too much of it would be physically weakening. It will not work positively without the refreshment of shorter wavelength colours, such as green or blue. If, for example, you wanted a predominantly Spring pink bedroom (in my experience, Spring women almost invariably find themselves attracted to the idea of a pink bedroom), you could choose a peach, so that you had a touch of yellow in the mix, and then contrast that with a light warm grey or green carpet, and floral curtains containing green leaves and blue flowers, with touches of the same peach, echoing the walls. If your partner is Autumn, however, please do not ask her or him to live with a grey carpet, anywhere in the house. Autumn has little, if any, true relationship with grey.

CHILDREN'S ROOMS

What about the children? So far we have only discussed adults reconciling their differences by mature debate. But children are unlikely to identify what is wrong with their room if the colours are not right and are probably more susceptible than adults, because they are relatively unconditioned. It is a misconception that, because children's immature eyes recognize bright primary colours first, they should always be surrounded by them. All too often loving parents will decorate the nursery in light, bright colours, which are much stronger than the colours in the rest of the house. Then they wonder why the child is hyperactive, or does not sleep easily. It is no accident that the traditional colours for new born babies' clothes are soft pastels – 'pink for a girl, blue for a boy' – (if the colour is supposed to focus on the gender, strictly speaking it should be 'red for a boy', but that would be far too demanding for a young baby).

Children need the balance of ease, as well as stimulation, just as adults do. It is fine to give them strongly coloured toys to play with and to help them to develop colour awareness, but when they go to bed they need soft, soothing colours.

It is tempting for parents to impose their own taste and experience on their children; it is human nature, but it must be resisted if harmony is to prevail in the family. If you are linked to Autumn, your ice-maiden Winter daughter will not be supported by your imposition of the golden tones or sludge greens which you find so supportive. Children have a natural sense of colour and form, which I strongly urge you to allow them to express and develop. As soon as they are old enough to point, consult them about colours you propose to use for them.

Later, when your rebellious teenager wants to paint his whole room black, or wants psychedelic mania in there, just understand that he needs to express the confusion and insecurity of adolescence, as he struggles to come to terms with the simultaneous arrival in his life of immense physical and emotional changes inside himself, and important educational landmarks to be achieved for the outside world. Don't be too hard on him.

As in any other sphere, reconciling differences is all about understanding attitudes and honest communication.

CHAPTER TEN

Yellow Bedrooms?

A friend of mine who owns a hotel telephoned me one day and invited me to go and stay for the weekend.

'Apart from the fact that I haven't seen you for a while, I've got a problem with one of the bedrooms, and I need your advice.'

Over tea when I arrived, she explained: being beside the sea, and beautifully appointed, the hotel was often used for conferences and it was their policy to offer conference organizers what is known as a 'facility visit' – a complimentary stay at the hotel, to judge at first hand the quality of service etc. There was one room which they sometimes used for these visits, but every guest who ever occupied it proved troublesome, and the only time that conference organizers did not book their event at the hotel was if one of them was occupying this particular bedroom. The whole staff was beginning to feel quite superstitious about it.

'It is as if it's jinxed!' my friend said.

I smiled to myself.

'Is it yellow?' I enquired.

The room overlooked not the sea but the courtyard, so it was not as light and bright as most of the other rooms. Being an experienced designer, my friend recognized the need to maximize the light, so she had chosen a very attractive bright yellow wallpaper. It was all quite beautifully done, but unfortunately, she had also chosen a yellow background for the floral-patterned matching bedcover and curtains. She had observed all the rules of interior design, and the quality of the fittings and finishes was exquisite – but she had overlooked the psychology of colour.

I explained to her that the reason her guests were grumpy was quite simple: they were not getting a decent night's sleep! Yellow is a stimulating colour and, as you will recall from Chapter Two, it relates to the emotions. Churned-up emotions, even if the stimulus is positive, are not conducive to sleep; in the morning, if you are the kind of person who prefers, as it were, to sneak up on the day and break yourself in gently, yellow is emotionally far too demanding. A judicious touch of it might contribute to the awakening process, but in this case there was imbalance, both in the amount of yellow used and in the chromatic intensity of the colour itself.

I advised my friend to keep the curtains and furnishings but change the wallpaper; we chose a soft warm blue which matched one of the colours in the floral pattern. It was not necessary to remove all the yellow – as explained, a touch of it would be useful in encouraging the guests to feel lively when they awoke in the morning. A combination of blue and

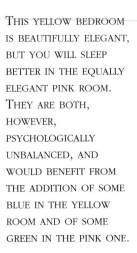

THIS YELLOW BEDROOM IS BEAUTIFULLY ELEGANT, BUT YOU WILL SLEEP BETTER IN THE EQUALLY ELEGANT PINK ROOM. THEY ARE BOTH, HOWEVER, PSYCHOLOGICALLY UNBALANCED, AND WOULD BENEFIT FROM THE ADDITION OF SOME BLUE IN THE YELLOW ROOM AND OF SOME GREEN IN THE PINK ONE.

THIS BATHROOM REFLECTS MELLOW AUTUMN. THE COLOURS ARE FROM THE COOLER END OF THE AUTUMN PALETTE, THE LINES ARE SUMMER. (THE DARK WOODEN LOO SEAT IS PURE AUTUMN.)

yellow, provided the particular shades chosen are right, present an excellent psychological balance.

The same applies to your home, but it is an even more important consideration there, as you are not just occupying your bedroom for a temporary visit. If you love yellow, and have set your heart on a yellow bedroom, then please – tone it down, either by using a very soft yellow which is not much more intense than a cream (cream is about 5–10 per cent yellow added to white) or by using it in small quantities, balanced with a restful blue or possibly a soft mauve or violet.

When considering the best colour for your bedroom, there are a number of questions you need to ask yourself. We have already touched on issues relating to shared bedrooms, but if you have a room of your own, you can decorate it any way you like, and it has been my experience that this is a healthy thing to do. Give some thought to the attitude you have to your bedroom, and how you use it. Is it a haven for you, to which you retreat whenever you need sanctuary? Or do you only go in there to sleep, and stay long enough to get dressed in the morning? Are you perhaps one of those people who actually work in your bedroom, seeing a large double bed as a perfect place to spread out lots of papers or whatever? Do you have a television in there, or a chair where you sit and read, so it is in some respects an extension of the sitting room? Do you live alone, or share? If the latter, how do you feel if flatmates or family go into your bedroom? Do you feel that your privacy has been invaded, or is everyone welcome? Do you play your music in there? Are you a healthy sleeper or an insomniac? Do you have trouble getting up in the morning, and always feel sluggish first thing? You should obviously, if this is the case, examine your diet and your lifestyle, but it may be easier – and it will indubitably help a bit – to change the colour scheme in your bedroom.

I have already explained about the physically restful properties of pink; it is worth reminding you that any tint or shade with little chromatic intensity in it is essentially more soothing than a stronger version of exactly the same hue. So, for example, pink soothes, whilst red (or vivid shocking pink) stimulates; soft sky blue will calm the troubled mind, a strong royal or flag blue will provide intellectual stimulation. It is advisable, therefore, to ensure that the predominant influence in the bedroom is either a tint or a low-intensity shade, to encourage you to go off to sleep peacefully at night, and that the secondary influence is stimulating enough for you to feel refreshed in the morning. In terms of value, tints – i.e. hues with plenty of white added – are psychologically expansive, whilst shades – hues with black added – encourage emotional contraction (and help you to centre yourself).

As a general rule of thumb, the classic advice that light colours recede and dark colours advance is very sound, and should always be borne in mind with awkward-shaped rooms or small spaces. You can make a wall appear to have been pushed back by several feet if you decorate it in a very light, shorter wavelength colour – the most recessive being light blue.

Light blue or light green are always a safe bet in the bedroom, as they are calming and refreshing, but of course, most people want a bedroom in which sexual activity will be encouraged and supported – in which case flesh tones, pink, red or orange will work excellently, provided you apply them carefully enough to avoid creating a strain. People often think that black is a very sexy colour and invest a small fortune in black satin sheets, or incorporate a lot of black in the bedroom decor. The sophistication of black lends a hint of decadence to this situation, but it is not likely to enhance the sexual union, unless one or both partners are very strongly Winter-linked. Remember in Chapter Eight I explained that black is total absorption; it is heavy and suppressive. Visually, it will not flatter the skin tones of a warm personality, and any permanent occupant, no matter what season, of a predominantly black bedroom is going to start feeling oppressed and sluggish eventually. Far from sexy. All in all, therefore, it would not be my recommendation.

THE BATHROOM

If you have a bathroom ensuite with your bedroom, then the most effective approach is to consider them as one. (I was once asked to devise a colour scheme for a couple who had literally had the wall between their bedroom and their bathroom removed. The bathroom suite itself was at odds with the colour scheme they wanted for their bedroom and it was very difficult to reconcile. I confess I wondered at the time if this was not taking togetherness too far.) Many of the same psychological factors apply to both rooms – most obviously the need for intimacy and privacy.

If the bathroom is a communal one, another question arises: is it the only bathroom in the house, and is there competition for it at certain times of the day? If so, consider featuring some touches of strong, stimulating colours, such as red, yellow, orange or bright greens, to keep everyone on their toes and discourage lingering. Using red itself may be an overstatement, but the fact remains that it increases the perception of the speed at which time is passing (a phenomenon demonstrated by fast food restaurants the world over).

If the situation is a little less hectic, you can afford to create a more soothing atmosphere in there. Colours which echo the tones of the sea – blues, turquoise, watery greens – are very popular in the bathroom, and I would endorse that; these tones have a quality of freshness and cleanliness which is entirely appropriate. Another approach might be to use pink, as it is the most intimate colour, and will support positive feelings about your own body. If you consider bathtime to be a pleasurable experience, rather than a practical necessity, and you want your bathroom to be a place of beauty, lending itself to candlelight, aromatherapy, soft music and possibly meditation, include some deep blue or purple in there somewhere.

THIS BEAUTIFUL BLUE
DINING ROOM WILL
IMPRESS DINNER GUESTS

... BUT EVERYONE WILL
ENJOY THEMSELVES IN
THE WARM GOLDEN
MOOD OF THIS ONE.

YOU CAN ALMOST SMELL THE BREAD BAKING IN THIS WARM KITCHEN! THE COLOURS ARE IDEAL FOR STIMULATING THE APPETITE AND CREATING A CONVIVIAL ATMOSPHERE.

CHAPTER ELEVEN

Food for Thought

Before you start to redecorate the kitchen, ask yourself the same sort of questions as you did about the bedroom and the bathroom. How do you feel about food? Do you enjoy cooking? Or are you (like me) one of those who regard making the dinner as a chore, but often, when at leisure, feel inspired to be very creative and produce something quite brilliant for no particular reason?

The whole psychology of food is very complex, and encompasses deeply entrenched attitudes towards your childhood, your family and the concept of nurturing, the quality of both that which you feel you received and that which you are required to offer.

There is a whole branch of psychiatry dedicated to the problems of eating disorders; anorexia nervosa and bulimia are extremely complex conditions which, in my experience, have little to do with the physical reality of food itself. Refusal to sustain and feed your body is making a very drastic statement indeed. Rejecting someone else's cooking is a potent means of rejecting the whole person and his or her emotional offerings to you. It is the ultimate rebellion, which is virtually impossible to counter. We are all familiar with the sight of anxious parents trying to persuade a small but recalcitrant child to 'eat up your greens', but we often do not recognize that exactly the same scenario is constantly re-enacted in adulthood, if childhood difficulties and much pain and hurt have never been successfully resolved.

Equally, the Eastern mystics believe that the feelings of the cook will be imparted in the food. If it has been lovingly prepared and cooked with an open-hearted, generous attitude it will taste so much better. Have you ever noticed that there are some people in your life for whom your cooking never goes wrong, whilst there are others who, every time they come to dinner, seem to put some kind of jinx on it? For example, if you are burning with suppressed resentment, it is hardly surprising that you burn the soup; nursing an inferiority complex will quite possibly contribute to a dish which is considerably inferior to your usual standards. Analyse in depth what your attitude is consistently – do you actually feel that you are a good cook, or do you need all the help you can get?

Whilst I am not claiming that colour psychology offers a cure-all for every problem, these complexities can be exacerbated or they can be helped and tempered by the colours in the kitchen.

Notwithstanding the above, it is probably advisable to keep sight of the simple fact that food and eating are essentially physical, and therefore best supported by the long wavelength colours, deriving from red – red itself, orange, peach, etc. If the cook is feeling hungry, he or she will probably produce a better meal. In Chapter Eight we touched on the relationship between orange and feelings of hunger; it would obviously therefore encourage the cook and all the participants in the meal to be surrounded by a balanced amount of the right orange.

A word of caution: kitchens inevitably get hot, so red should be used very carefully, and properly balanced. I would not recommend using blue in a domestic kitchen to counter that perception of heat, as it will suppress the physical hunger and possibly quench the desire to produce a wonderful meal; also, if you have one of those large kitchens where everyone tends to congregate, blue is not particularly convivial; green would be a much better choice to cool down the atmosphere.

Yellow is an excellent choice for the kitchen, because it encourages creativity and optimism and it lightens the atmosphere.

THE DINING ROOM

There are obvious similarities between the mood of the kitchen and that of the dining room, as they are both focused on food and eating. However, the atmosphere in the dining room is ideally more relaxed and leisurely. It would be better to exclude yellow, as emotional stimulation is not particularly good for the digestion. Although blue is not generally physical, use of it in the dining room could be soothing, and particularly beneficial to anyone who suffers from chronic heartburn or acid indigestion. I would not recommend blue in a commercial restaurant, but in your home you can tailor your colour schemes to the individual requirements of the family.

You could balance the blue with a more physical secondary colour, so that the whole family, or guests, are not too inhibited.

If you entertain frequently, you should have a colour scheme which will encourage lively conversation, but do not overdo it. As in the kitchen, derivatives of red and orange are always effective. This is especially so if your dining room is rather draughty, or the central heating is not as good as it should be – under these circumstances it is difficult enough to warm up a dinner party.

It used to be that the one time of day when families spent any time together, and communicated, was around the dinner table, but these days, when the pace of life is so much more hectic, and mother is less likely to provide the corner-stone of the home, this does not happen nearly so frequently. All the generations tend to make their own independent arrangements, and often sit down to eat in front of the ubiquitous television set. It is therefore worth spending time and trouble to make the dining room, and mealtimes, as attractive as possible to the whole family. It is amazing what tensions can be dispelled over a relaxed – and delicious – meal.

THIS BLUE WOULD WORK
BETTER
PSYCHOLOGICALLY IF THE
CUSHIONS WERE IN
BALANCING TONES —
PEACH, ORANGE, CREAM
OR PINK. THE COOL
ELEGANCE OF THE
COLOURS IS ALSO AT
ODDS WITH THE
MAGNIFICENT AUTUMNAL
FIREPLACE AND MIRROR.

A YELLOW HALL WILL
GIVE ALL WHO ARRIVE AT
THE FRONT DOOR A
WARM, BRIGHT WELCOME.

CHAPTER TWELVE

Sitting Pretty

It is probably fair to say that virtually any colour will work in the sitting room, or general living area, because of the diversity of attitudes towards this part of the home. Until recent times, the rich in their large houses had different rooms for different activities – the music room, the library, the morning room, the boudoir, etc. – and the poor, with perhaps only one room in the entire house, were not concerned with the finer points of interior design. It is only in the twentieth century that homes became smaller and more flexible without necessarily indicating poverty. As a result interior design has become much more complicated.

If you view your sitting room essentially as a place where you welcome guests and you want to encourage stimulating conversation in that room most of the time, then a fairly strong yellow would work well, but be aware that it will not be a particularly relaxing room if you do not pay sufficient attention to the crucial issue of balance.

It may be that this part of your home provides sweet sanctuary, and the opportunity to sink into a chair and put your feet up after a long, demanding day. In this case, soft blues and greens would be very supportive.

If your marriage is going through a difficult phase, or you have a tense relationship with a particular member of the family, and this is the common ground on which you most often meet, the sweet calming properties of pink, or soft blue, will be the most helpful. Be wary of using red in a potential war zone!

If it is your habit to meditate in the living room, make sure there is some violet somewhere, to encourage you to centre yourself and take your mind to a higher plane. (The right tones of yellow and violet can present a wonderful basis for a balanced colour scheme.) Orange is a popular choice for the cushions on lotus chairs and other meditation aids, but I confess I do not understand why – beyond the symbolic association with the sun (yellow) and the life force (red) which governs the use of orange by the Hare Krishna movement and followers of Rajneesh and other Eastern gurus. The most powerful holy man in India – Sri Sathya Sai Baba – wears orange or red robes himself, but his followers do not. I am reliably informed that there is a very simple reason for this: as a young man, he wore traditional white, as his followers still do. The reason he changed was that he is only five feet four inches tall, and as his following grew to millions across the world it became difficult for people to see him in the huge crowds. Those who looked after him were concerned that they often lost sight of him, so they prevailed upon him to adopt more highly visible colours. As we know, orange is an extrovertive colour, and it would not be my recommendation that it be used to support the concept of spiritual or psychological meditation.

It is not unknown for people to transfer virtually any activity into the living room, from shelling peas in comfort to mending a motorbike when it is pouring with rain outside. (I could not begin to recommend colours to support either of these latter.)

IS YOUR SACRED COW REALLY SACRED?

More often than not it is the sitting room which presents the biggest interior design challenges. Often the essentials are already built in to the kitchen and bedrooms, so you do not have to furnish them beyond a table or a bed, but the sitting room requires much more effort. It is unusual for anyone to time things so perfectly that the whole room is completely revamped at the same time. We are not often afforded the opportunity to decorate, carpet and furnish an entirely empty space from scratch. Usually when you first move into a house or flat, you have scraped the bottom of the barrel to find the money to buy the best home you can afford, and then you are confronted by the horrors of stamp duty, removal costs, legal fees, etc.

Even if you have the funds to remodel the house or flat, carry out structural alterations and redecoration, the chances are you will have brought furniture with you, which still has life in it, and you cannot afford, or do not wish, to dispose of it. Sometimes good quality carpeting, and possibly curtains too, are included in the sale and it would be criminal to throw them out. Later, when you can afford to change the carpet, the furniture will have a few years left in it, or the curtains will still be going strong. The timing is so often out.

The most common problems which people present for my advice concern this dilemma. There always seems to be a 'sacred cow' which cannot be ignored, be it the carpet, an expensive sofa, even a table that has been handed down for generations. The existing carpet may be brown and the incoming three-piece suite blue, an unbalanced colour combination, as both are serious and potentially introvertive, suppressive colours; alternatively, both the curtains and the upholstery may be vividly patterned.

My advice is always: first, let us re-examine the 'sacred cow'. How sacred is it? No matter how good the quality, if the carpeting is in a strong colour which is negative for you, it is not worth trying to create a home around it, and live with the inevitably negative influence. If you cannot afford to replace it, it might even be better to consider taking it up and staining the floorboards, investing in a few inexpensive rugs – any alternative to trying to force your lifestyle and personality to fit a carpet. If it is the suite which is the rogue element, consider re-upholstering it or, a cheaper alternative, using loose covers – perhaps you could find throw rugs or blankets in wonderful colours to fling over it.

Once we have resolutely taken a lateral view of the problem and thought it through thoroughly, if it is decided that the 'sacred cow' is genuinely sacred, there will always be a colour solution which, whilst perhaps not perfect, will improve the situation in the short term, while you work towards the ideal. Happily, carpets are not often in very strong colours, but more neutral tones, so you can find a way to harmonize the room so as to reduce awareness of it. It is often a question of balance again. The colour balance in a room will materially alter the perceptions.

For example, going back to our brown carpet and blue suite, walls papered or painted yellow, with some bright cushions echoing the same yellow, will go a long way towards lifting and balancing the mood, as there will now be more yellow than either brown or blue. If the carpet is the only problem, you may find a print for the curtains which contains a touch of the colour of the carpet, but a much larger percentage of colours which are more positive for you. Textiles are rarely 100 per cent accurate in their seasonal colour combinations and, provided a print contains 70–80 per cent colours in your season, you can be positively supported by it.

Finally, remember what I pointed out in Chapter Four about peach, turquoise and cream: these colours have versions which straddle the borderlines between all four seasons and can be considered as a useful means of drawing disparate colours together.

If there is a room available which is not required to be a bedroom, it is always a good idea to equip it as a kind of extra sitting room. The Americans consider a 'den' to be an absolute essential in any family home. In Britain, we tend to call it a 'study'. If one of the family actually works from home, then the study might amount to a fully equipped office; if not, it may be little more than an extra room, with perhaps a desk in it and a sofa bed, possibly the TV, where anyone who needs a bit of privacy can go. If this is the room where the paperwork is taken care of, or any kind of studying or homework is done, the best colour would probably be a mid to darkish blue – introvertive and intellectually soothing, to encourage clear thought and quiet concentration.

The other challenging area is often the hall. This is where yellow really comes into its own, especially if the hallway is narrow and dark, as they so often are. The perception of sunshine will give all who arrive at the front door a warm, bright welcome and create the optical illusion of a larger space.

PART FOUR

THE FOUR SEASONS AT WORK

CHAPTER THIRTEEN

Square Pegs

Some years ago, I worked briefly as a careers advisor, and I was constantly fascinated by people's attitudes to work. Work, as opposed to 'having a job', was not (and often still is not) considered important in itself, merely as a means of earning money. This, despite the reality that our work is often the driving force of our entire lives; it takes up more than half our waking hours in purely chronological terms, and determines how we are perceived by society. In those days, sexism was still rampant, so a large percentage of the young women I saw – particularly, it has to be said, upper-crust young women, who were expected to 'marry well' – were given the stark choice:

'Do you want to go to secretarial college, or do a Cordon Bleu?'

Often, having just achieved good grades at 'A' level, they were understandably frustrated at the assumption that it was not really an option for them to go to university. Of course, there were many women who did go to university, but it was not automatically considered the norm.

In the case of young men, it was assumed that they would more or less follow in parental footsteps – doctors bred doctors, architects bred designers of one kind or another, actors bred theatrical dynasties and the sons of financiers automatically went into the City.

It is often assumed that this is an indication of genetic characteristics, handed down. I suggest that this is not necessarily the case at all, but rather a matter of familiarity and conditioning. If, for example, you have been brought up in a home where the parents live and breathe the theatre, and their friends are theatrical luminaries, you will inevitably absorb much of that atmosphere yourself, so that when you apply to drama school, or audition for a part, you already know what is required and feel at home in that situation.

Sheer propinquity determines the high proportion of people who marry someone in the same line of work as themselves, so family conversation is often built around the parents' jobs; a medical family tends to talk about medical matters, writers might argue about syntax. This conditioning runs very deep and it takes a strong-minded child to swim against that tide. Conversely, a truly talented artist, or actor, comes up against a barrage of opposition if he or she belongs to a family of accountants, miners, police officers, teachers:

'Why can't you get a proper job?'

I even know one actress manqué (a star still, in her local amateur circuit) whose father said, when asked if daughter could try for drama school,

'I always suspected it: you have the mind of a pantry maid! I suggest you think of something more serious.'

Another client had always wanted to be a teacher, but her mother had trained and worked as such herself until her marriage, and hated every minute of it – her opposition was implacable.

There is confusion about the criteria for choosing a career. No account is taken of personality type and the fundamental needs and interests (which drive ability and success) of each individual. It is generally thought that the best way to decide is by some simple equation worked out on the basis of money, hours, status and availability of jobs. All of these are obviously relevant, to a greater or lesser degree, but the really important factors – job content, natural ability, satisfaction, personal growth and genuine contribution to the greater good – are discounted.

To compound the problem, society then goes on to classify and value people solely on the basis of their jobs. One of the first questions we ask each other when we are introduced is 'What do you do?' and then we are likely to miss an opportunity to know someone really interesting as we dismiss them on the basis of our thoughtless interpretations:

'I'm an accountant.' ('Boring.')
'I'm a hairdresser.'('Brainless.')
'I'm a traffic warden.' ('Fascist.)
'I'm a road sweeper.' ('No interest to me.')
'I'm a doctor.' ('Thinks he's God.')
'I'm a film director.' ('Poser.')
'I'm a politician.' ('She's lying.')
'I'm an estate agent.' ('Can't be trusted.')

It is unrealistic, given these widespread attitudes, to expect anyone to make the right decision, just at the point in life where the most confusion reigns. In adolescence we have little experience of a world outside our own immediate surroundings, and we do not know the implications – even the existence – of a myriad of choices available. In many cases, there is a strong negative recognition: 'I don't know what I want to do for the rest of my life – I just know what I don't want.' The pressure is on; we are insecure, and keenly aware that the time has come to confront the Big Wide World and become self-sufficient, so we opt for the apparently most attractive, or least frightening, option. We are extremely lucky if we find the right career first time. Consequently, most people spend the first ten, twenty or more years after they complete their education in the wrong job.

At that point, we have a crisis – in our forties, it is so common as to be the acknowledged, almost universal, condition known as 'mid-life crisis', and it seems to be happening earlier and earlier – as awareness grows that we have not got our lives right. Courageous souls will make the terrifying decision to change, but most will not, preferring to devote their energy to coming to terms with what they have got.

People who are happy in their work are a joy to behold. They rarely watch the clock, being mostly unaware of time, they are good humoured and dedicated way beyond the point of mere duty. They may not set the world on fire, but they are very good at their jobs and are usually happy and successful in most areas of their lives. If we question such people, we will often find that they came upon their career by accident – a stroke of sheer luck Alternatively it was either something they knew absolutely that they wanted to do, to the exclusion of all other ideas, right from early childhood before they even had a very clear idea of what it entailed, or it was the result of a complete change of direction, taken in maturity.

Until recently, applicants for any job were judged on the basis of qualifications and the ability to write a good resumé of their career to date and present themselves effectively at interview. There is no doubt that impressive qualifications and training are all to the good. However, training is a poor second to talent in the determining of long-term success; often the most successful people are self-taught. My teacher in California observed rather drily one day,

'With the possible exception of brain surgeons, I have to say I do not really approve of training.'

At the time, I was rather shocked and did not understand the point she was making, but on reflection I realized that training can often consist of a mechanical memorizing, or observing, of other people's way of doing things, built on the assumption that your way could not be better. Yet of the six most prolific inventors currently employed by ICI, five have never been to university! If you happen to be a genius, but you have not yet discovered it, you may defer to the greater experience of the teacher, who in fact is less talented than you are, to the detriment of your own progress and understanding. There is a difference between a teacher (or any other person) with thirty years' experience and a teacher with one year's experience, repeated thirty times.

Recognition is growing that something more than formal qualifications is required; an aptitude for presentation is not necessarily the best qualification for every job. I know of at least one university which is addressing the question of what precisely talent is, and whether it can be defined and analysed. Personnel directors are adopting new ways to determine what kind of person an applicant really is, and what makes him or her tick. Psychometric tests and such techniques as graphology (handwriting analysis) – even astrology – are used throughout industry and commerce.

If you give some thought to the question of what type of person you really are, and acknowledge where your strengths and weaknesses may lie, before you decide on possible careers, you are more likely to succeed in finding your niche. You will score highly on aptitude tests and the whole process will run more smoothly. Alternatively, you may be already settled into a career and not entirely happy, but unable to put your finger on what is wrong. If this section helps you to see where the problem lies, you may be able to make adjustments without too drastic a change.

FINDING THE BEST OUTLET FOR YOUR TALENTS

From what I wrote in Part Two, it is clear that the infinite permutations of typical characteristics in each of the four personality types, which go to make each person the unique individual that every single one of us is, preclude a simple list of careers for each group. Your talents are uniquely your own, and you know best how to deploy them. However, the chances are, as we have already established, that you are not aware of, or perhaps just not sufficiently secure in, this knowledge, and an examination of the archetypes will help you.

The idea that your colouring, colour preferences and the personality that they reflect will predispose you to shine in a particular field of endeavour may seem rather far-fetched, but the fact remains that colouring and colour preferences do give us very clear insights into the essential nature of a person, which are extremely relevant to your career.

Once more let us consider the archetypes, and let me remind you of the influence of subordinate seasons. Also, please remember the trap of subjective interpretation, which it is all too easy to fall into. To describe something as cold, for example, may suggest a negative perception, but if you were stuck in the desert at high noon the concept of cold would be the most attractive idea in the world – so the adjectives I shall use are not judgements, just relative descriptions.

In the workplace, it is also important to understand that, whilst the typical characteristics of a season may be the predominant factor driving a person' s life, we all ideally have a balance of all the characteristics, just as we have all the spectral hues in our personal palette. It is a matter of emphasis. For example, if a Winter executive usually uses his intellect and logic to make decisions, this does not mean that he is unfeeling; the consistently caring attitude of Spring does not mean that he cannot think clearly and logically – all the characteristics described are entirely relative, so do not jump to conclusions.

SPRING

The essence of springtime in the wild is the return of light, sunshine and warmth, after the long, dark months. It is about regeneration, new beginnings, high energy, excitement. Spring linked people are essentially extrovert. You may be rather shy, and consider yourself introvert, but it is not so – you will always be externally motivated. You respond quickly to external circumstances and other people, even if the response is to shy away. You have great charm, and you like to be popular.

One of the best areas for you is the world of hotels, leisure and tourism. Spring has a terrific knack of generating excitement and creating the impression that where you are is 'where it's at'. You lighten the atmosphere, and you are fun. A very strong Summer subordinate may keep this fun side of you sedately under cover for years, but it is there. Your laughter is light and infectious – I cannot ever remember encountering a Spring-linked person who did not have a sense of humour. This will stand you in good stead when the air-traffic controllers are on strike and you have 150 tired tourists to look after, or the hot water system in your hotel has failed at 8 a.m. You genuinely care for the welfare of your clients or guests and they will recognize that. You are naturally attracted to the sea and the seaside. In fact, a career in the navy might also appeal to you for that reason (but not as a submariner – Spring personalities often have a tendency to claustrophobia).

The ability to generate excitement is obviously useful in any enterprise concerned with promoting ideas, products or a service – i.e. sales and marketing or advertising. You are quick-witted, with a natural talent for communication and for 'thinking on your feet'. You are unlikely to concern yourself unduly with the how and why, and you are not happy when things proceed too slowly, no matter how justified the measured pace may be; patience is not a strong feature of your personality. Your enthusiasm will get things done quickly, and you are keen to tell the world about the achievements of your company/client/product. You like to be out and about, not tied down.

One of the best secretaries I ever knew was a Bandbox Spring lady. Her crisp personality and awesome efficency owed much to her Winter subordinate influence, but her lovely Spring warmth charmed everyone and enabled her to protect her boss from unwelcome demands without offence. She could get away with being extremely outspoken, just because she had the knack of saying things lightly and she had a ready smile.

As I mentioned in Part Two, your naturally caring attitude will stand you in good stead as a nurse; your positive approach will always make people feel better.

Another area for you to consider is any kind of work involving children. You have a natural affinity with the young, all the way through your life, and you can always find sufficient reserves of physical energy to help you keep up with them. You know instinctively how to approach a child, and never make the common mistake of talking down to him or her. Nursery nursing, child guidance and teaching (any age group) would all be good fields for you to consider.

If you decide to be a teacher, do not dismiss the possibility of teaching sport – you probably enjoy sports, you definitely enjoy being out of doors and you would be good at generating the enthusiasm which is so often lacking in schoolchildren who are not keen to go out in the cold in the middle of a winter's day to play games.

Being tied to any repetitive task, working alone, a very quiet atmosphere, inflexible routines, meeting rigid deadlines – these are all factors which would cause the light of enthusiasm to die in the eyes of a Spring-linked personality. You need people as much as you need air, you need flexibility and visible objectives. You enjoy a busy atmosphere and respond instantly to a sudden rush. You are a good team player. Running a restaurant would be good for you, as long as you were out front, and the restaurant was successful enough to ensure that it never got too quiet.

In the theatre, or films, you will be particularly good at comedy, musical or otherwise. A typical example of irrepressible Spring is Dame Judi Dench, one of the British theatre's greatest actresses. At the same time as she is honoured and respected for her classical work in the theatre, she is even better known for the comic sitcoms she does so brilliantly on TV.

Spring is a natural dancer, and likely to be able to sing. In the relief of the 1950s, when the world was coming out of the austerity and gloom of World War II, a mood of optimism and a sense of new beginnings swept through society everywhere. The whole world wanted to celebrate. This was particularly reflected in the Hollywood musicals of the period, when such stars as Doris Day, Shirley Jones and Jane Powell – all Spring-linked – came into their own, as had Spring Ginger Rogers in the 1930s. (It is said that the latter used to become very resentful and impatient with Winter-linked Fred Astaire's ruthless perfectionism – when her feet were literally bleeding – but how wonderfully effective the combination was!)

Finally, every company reception area should ideally be staffed by Spring, whose interest in all comers will not flag. Spring will smile and be helpful through thick and thin.

SUMMER

In many ways, you are exactly opposite to Spring in your needs and talents, although you have the same delicacy and lightness of touch. Your greatest joy is to bring order out of chaos and you welcome the opportunity to do so, preferably uninterrupted. You are gentle and perceptive, although essentially introverted, and you are uncomfortable with over-statement in anything.

You are a natural peacemaker and your nurturing instinct is strong, so the personnel department would be a good arena for you. In times of strife, a Summer-linked person knows best how to pour oil on troubled waters and arbitrate. You will be endlessly patient in the long drawn-out process of, for example, trades union negotiation. International diplomacy would benefit from your talents. Your innate sense of balance would also be supported by work in accountancy or book-keeping. The law is another area which would fulfil this need. You are very straight.

If you worked as a doctor – physician or GP – you would find that the combination of gentle nurturing and calm assessment of facts which occurs naturally in you would enable you to offer your patients the very best treatment, without getting carried away with emotion. You keep your cool, but your sensitivity would be of enormous help to the distressed. Obviously nursing would be good for you too. You could also run the hospital with quiet efficiency as an administrator.

You have an inherent respect for quality and particularly respond to it in art, music, antiques or books. Just about anything in this field – artist, art dealer, librarian or publisher – would be good for you. You almost certainly have musical ability and you are a natural conservationist.

Although you find the hurlyburly of a busy workplace slightly stressful – unlike Spring, you do not thrive on it – you can, nevertheless, shut it out and create order and peace in your own particular area. We had a manageress at the hotel, in my youth, who was a gem. She had already been running the hotel for some years before my family bought it and fortunately my parents had the brains to realize that it was a good idea to keep her on. Other people, who could not see beyond her quiet shyness and unswerving dedication to routine, were quick to suggest that she did not have enough sparkle for the hotel business and should be dismissed. As my mother so trenchantly put it,

'I can sparkle to order, and we are not short of people who can look after the front of house – what is missing is solid reliability behind the scenes. This lady knows what she is doing, and we need her.'

She was proved right a month later, on New Year's Day; a ball had taken place the previous night and everyone had been sparkling their socks off until 4 a.m., so no one was up to much the next morning. The hotel was full and – although she had found the previous evening's revelry slightly shocking – the manageress was on duty at 6.30 a.m. as usual, ensuring that all the guests' bills were ready and calmly carrying on with the essentials.

You could set your watch by this lady's routine and people were inclined to be rather disparaging about it – but what a treasure she was! The books always balanced, the stocktaking was always accurate and everyone knew where they were; her loyalty was absolute. She was an archetypal Summer, with her greying hair and blue, blue eyes, her straight back and her gentle smile. She had a wonderful way of dealing with staff problems. The hotel world is very pressured and the kind of people who are good at dealing with the general public can be rather excitable. It often happened that two of them would burst into her office saying,

'It's no good! I can't work with her – either she goes or I do!'

Completely unruffled, she would smile sweetly and say,'I see. Well, I am rather busy at the moment, so I suggest you go away, decide between yourselves which of you is leaving and which staying, and let me know.'

Needless to say, she rarely heard any more about it.

What would truly distress you would be a boss who pushed you into the limelight, who tried to get you to perform heavy selling techniques, whose business methods were at all questionable (although you would be loyal and never 'spill the beans', you would not be happy), or who was boorish and insensitive. You are, as previously mentioned, by no means a wimp, so you probably would not stay long in such a negative situation, but you would find it very difficult to deal with.

Floristry is another wonderful career for you; you love flowers and are a born artist.

Ironically, the idea of becoming an actor is not something for you to dismiss. Very successful actors are often painfully shy; adopting a different persona on stage or film presents you with an opportunity to protect your real self, and you would be well able to keep your private life out of the limelight. I think that one of our finest actors, Sir Alec Guinness, must be Summer-linked, as he is so typical. You would be wonderful behind the scenes too, in the wardrobe department, props, make-up or one of the technical areas.

AUTUMN

Autumn likes to delve. Any form of scientific research or detection interests you. You would make an excellent police officer, provided you could keep your rebellious tendencies in check – you are not terribly conformist by nature. In the armed forces your instinct to protect the underdog and fight injustice wherever you saw it would help you to come to terms with the unquestioning obedience so essential in the military. You are happy to conform when you understand the reasons for it.

I mentioned in Part One that you would have a problem with objectivity if you worked as a lawyer; in fact the ideal situation in that area would be for you to be a solicitor or legal executive in litigation or criminal work, gathering all the evidence and building a solid case, before handing it to a Winter-linked barrister, whose talent would be in distilling it with the utmost objectivity and presenting it with precision and dramatic flair.

In the medical field your forte would be in the area of psychoanalysis, psychology or psychiatry, but almost any aspect of medicine would be good for you, with your endless fascination for investigation and your love of people. You would be unlikely to dismiss complementary medicine, and probably know a lot about it, even if you are not working in a medical field and it is nothing to do with your profession. In fact, the whole New Age interests you – you might be sceptical and you will question it, but you are unlikely to make the mistake of dismissing absolutely the possibility of any concept, simply because it is beyond your current level of understanding.

You have a natural affinity with animals; autumnal people make excellent vets. Indeed you are more a rural creature than an urban one yourself. You may live and work in the city, but you will always hanker after the country – hence the high incidence of weekend country cottages bought by autumnal city-dwellers in Britain.

Anything which enables you to dig, either metaphorically, as a researcher or a detective, or literally, as a miner, an archaeologist or an explorer of some kind, would be good for you. You would also flourish in the world of antique dealing.

Like Spring, you are externally motivated, but you are more likely to lose yourself and your awareness of others in your work, if it is of sufficient interest to you. Consequently, you can work alone more readily than Spring – but when the work is finished you need, more than most, to tell the world about it, so you should be aware of the danger of taking your work home with you, and not being able to switch off. You could have a tendency to get too emotional about issues. Still, you are a great crusader.

Fund-raising and charity work are areas where your lack of detachment can be turned to good use. Will anyone who saw it on television ever forget Autumn Bob Geldof's passionate plea for support, when the funds slowed down halfway through Live Aid day? Nobody but an Autumn-linked person could have devised and pushed that concept through to fruition with such spectacular success as he did. Both Terry Wogan and Sue Cook are autumnal, and they are obviously in their element as they persuade us to part with millions for Children in Need every year. Esther Rantzen's Childline, Lenny Henry's Comic Relief, Sophia Loren's tireless charity work for the United Nations and Mother Teresa's extraordinary self-sacrifice among the poor of India – the list of autumnal personalities working to change the world is very long.

Autumn has a restless energy, which must be channelled effectively, if trouble is to be avoided. It is unrealistic to expect the Autumn-linked woman, for instance, to work exclusively at home, looking after her house and her family, without some absorbing hobby. Most Autumn-linked women have careers outside the home and are good at juggling competing demands.

You are likely to be attracted to the theatre, or film. It is interesting to note the way the latter has changed through the twentieth century. In the earlier years, up to about the beginning of the 1960s, the 'Star System' applied, especially in Hollywood. The film industry revolved around major film studios, who simply signed up the actors to a contract, usually of seven years, during which they were not required to contribute in any way to decisions affecting their own careers, but had to play whatever parts they were given. The studios chose actors with recognizable 'star quality' and then made stars of them. They took care of every little detail of their lives, including if necessary paying for cosmetic dentistry or surgery. The star's image was all, and the studio had legions of high-powered PR people protecting it.

This system basically worked better for the pragmatism of Winter-linked personalities than for Autumn, so many of the stars of those early years were Winter-linked – Clark Gable, Gregory Peck, Robert Taylor, John Wayne, Joan Crawford, Marlene Dietrich, Hedi Lamarr, Vivien Leigh. All four seasons were represented, of course – Autumn Katharine Hepburn and Bette Davis, Summer Greta Garbo and Gary Cooper, Spring Carole Lombard and Ginger Rogers – but far and away the majority of stars were Winter-linked.

Eventually, the actors began to assert their individuality more strongly. The whole approach to acting known as Method, requiring that more thought be put into the motivation behind a character, rather than its presentation, came in, and the focus gradually shifted. Actors began to express the creative need to be involved in the whole process and it became much less unthinkable that an actor could produce and/or direct a film. Autumn warmth and passion came into their own – in the last thirty years or so the whole industry has been dominated by Autumn-linked actors – Dustin Hoffman, Kevin Costner, Robin Williams, Kenneth Branagh, Robert Redford, Clint Eastwood, Meryl Streep (very strong Summer subordinate), Jane Fonda, Glenn Close, Barbra Streisand, Bette Midler.

The point of this digression is to remind you of the importance to Autumn of substance, rather than style; your image has to reflect reality. You are fundamentally averse to feeling restricted, either physically or – more likely – psychologically, and you need to express yourself. If you decide to seek a career in the film industry or the theatre, you will find the whole process, not just the performance, of immense interest and value to you.

Your iconoclastic questioning could lead you to success as a journalist, a satirist or perhaps a cartoonist. You also have a powerful imagination, so creative writing would be a good choice for you.

Your extrovert character could make for success in sales and marketing, but for you belief in the product is essential. You are not going to be happy just following a clever script to help you sell something. If you believe in it, your conviction will carry the day more effectively than the best thought-out sales talk, but if you do not believe in it, forget it – you will not make the targets.

WINTER

The great strength of Winter is your ability to keep your eye on the ball. You do not lose sight of the objectives of any enterprise. You are naturally efficient, with a talent for clear thinking and logic. Your innate sense of drama is invaluable in any presentation – artistic, theatrical or promotional.

I remember an incident once which demonstrates Winter's view of work: I was visiting a successful catering company, and my visit happened to coincide with the arrival of a Health and Safety inspector.

'Your rest area is not as good as it could be,' he said to the boss, a brilliantly artistic patissier who achieved awesome levels of productivity, both for himself and his staff, by sheer efficiency and single-minded dedication.

'What?' he responded, obviously mystified. 'But I don't pay people to come here to rest, I pay them to come here to work!'

He was perfectly serious, and before you decide that the man was a cold-hearted, exploitive boss, it should be said that he himself worked harder than any three of his employees put together, and his staff were very loyal to him.

Winter will always turn up on time – lack of punctuality irritates you, and you cannot understand why people are so cavalier in their attitude towards it.

You have the knack of seeing the broader picture, which enables you to take an overview and delegate effectively; you always achieve a neat balance, in that you can see the whole picture without being diverted from your objectives. Therefore, you will do your work well and focus all your energy on to it, regardless of whether you are enjoying it or not; you are very disciplined. If you are in a subservient position, you will not become terribly hot under the collar about your rights and what everybody else is doing – you will simply get on with the job. You will, however, have ensured at the outset that the terms and conditions under which you work are crystal clear. You are not particularly interested in what other people think of you – the standards you set for yourself are higher than anyone else would set for you anyway.

The fields that will attract you and benefit from your special talents are: financial institutions, banking, stockbroking, commodity trading, where your razor-sharp calculations will give you the edge; politics – probably leaning more towards the Right than the Left; Chief Executive of just about any industrial concern; fashion; film and theatre – often in the vanguard of experimental work, such as that of Winter-linked Steven Berkoff; public relations; architecture; design of any kind – fashion, interiors, textiles, product or graphic. If you decide to go into medicine, the best area for you would be surgery, where your precision with the scalpel would be second to none.

In the fashion world, the inherent drama of your personality would lend itself with great success to modelling, and you would not mind the negative aspects of the job, such as boredom and impersonal dealings with people, cameras etc. You would love the catwalk, as you slink or imperiously stride along it, above the eye level of the audience, so that they are all looking up at you; nobody can do it as well as Winter.

As I briefly mentioned in the section about Autumn, if you go into the law, the best area of it for you would be as a barrister. You will inevitably become a judge (there is no doubt about that!) and your objectivity will stand you, and the legal system, in very good stead. You will also not find it necessary to air your personal opinions when delivering a judgement, so we will all be spared lurid tabloid headlines about controversial judges who are insensitive and out of touch with the 'real world'. (It seems to me that judges see the 'real world' being played out in front of them every working minute.)

Your surroundings are important to you – there is likely to be a high percentage of Winter-linked people working in, for example the essentially avant garde Lloyds building or the new Channel Four building in London, both Richard Rogers designed, aspirational places which reflect ideas for the future. You would be drawn to them instinctively. You are essentially an urban creature. Even if you were born and bred in the country (as indeed millions of Winter-linked oriental people are) you are sophisticated and you will always be attracted to the city.

There is one point about social service, in its broadest sense, which is worth explaining: you would be very good at it, but you would not particularly enjoy it. Let me give you an example: some years ago, four women, including myself, were working together. Two of us were autumnal, one was linked to Spring and the fourth to Winter. The going was quite tough, and at one point the other Autumn-linked woman broke down in tears. To

our surprise, the dam burst and she spilled out a barrage of emotion, fear, anger and pain. I noticed that the Spring-linked woman's eyes were filling with tears, and I could feel a lump in my own throat. Neither of us said a word, but stood transfixed. With no evidence of emotion, the Winter-linked woman stepped forward and gently touched her distressed colleague's arm, saying exactly the right thing to help her to recover. Had she not been there, it is quite possible that, in our well-intentioned sympathy, the other three of us might have wallowed in unproductive emotion for the rest of the day.

Whilst you have the capacity to detach yourself from excessive emotion, you would find it draining to be confronted by it all day long – as social workers, nurses, and other care workers on the front line inevitably are.

Personal responsibility is high on your list of priorities, and you allow subordinates and colleagues the space and opportunity to take responsibility for themselves too. Although you are autocratic, you are too big a character ever to indulge in petty jealousies or unnecessary competition. You love one of your own team to succeed. When you delegate, you have no need to keep looking over the person's shoulder as they work, because you are able to give them the freedom to do a good job and assume that they will, until or unless it proves otherwise – in which case you will be very tough.

The important factor in all of the above is to be aware, perhaps even more than you recognize what you *can* do well, of what factors would really go against your grain. Your subordinate characteristics will exert considerable influence, but some things are fundamental. Spring cannot cope with repetitive work, alone, in a badly lit place. Summer shrinks from the limelight. Autumn hates to be restricted or fobbed off with trivia. Winter will accept most things if the prospects are good, but is not at his best in any kind of squalid enterprise or place.

CHAPTER FOURTEEN

The Working Environment

In choosing colours for the workplace, the same knotty question arises: with four different types likely to be working together, what colours will support them all?

There are two elements to the answer. The theme emphasized in Part Two and running through this whole book is that the one universally attractive characteristic, instantly recognizable and not subject to the influence of intellect, conditioning or subjectivity, is authenticity. Therefore designing the working environment in one season, properly balanced and entirely true to itself, will create a harmonious atmosphere to which everyone will respond.

Deciding on which season to use brings us to the other element: in interior design, the key factor in successful use of colour is psychological mode. This idea will be explained further in the section on commercial design, but it is about using colours to focus on the aspect of a person which is in play in any given situation. For example, a person in the boardroom will be in an entirely different psychological mode from the same person in the bedroom.

So science laboratories are usually decorated in clinical white and a Winter decor – which encourages the objectivity and reasoning so vital to scientific success – whilst everyone recognizes instinctively that a boutique selling lingerie is most appropriately decorated in soft Summer tones of pink and blue or grey.

These are oversimplifications, of course. The reality is that we find enormous variation across workplaces in the same field. In practice what usually happens is that the personality of the most senior person involved in the decision process will determine the colour scheme. It may or may not be entirely appropriate, but this simple, distinctly unscientific, approach will tell us much more about the company and its underlying philosophy than is often realized – if we know what to look for. The point is that the most senior person involved in that decision is obviously likely to be in a position to wield considerable influence on other factors which determine the nature of the company, so his or her colour choices will tell you what to expect. The boss's attitudes will permeate down through the whole company, and those attitudes can be clearly identified by looking at the colours in the workplace. It is worth having a good look before you decide to join them.

Two examples come to mind: a very large accountancy firm in London spends a lot of money promoting its image as a caring company which places much emphasis on training and encouraging young people into the profession, although this is not the way it is generally perceived. It has a large building which was recently refurbished, but the colour scheme was not changed, just renewed, in almost pure Winter. This is not necessarily a bad thing – Winter is very aspirational and focuses on material considerations, efficiency and reliability. It could be exactly the right choice for a large accountancy practice.

The problem with this building is that whilst the walls and the floor in the reception area are done in warm-toned marble, the rest of the building is carpeted in grey; the panels used to divide up all the space into individual workstations are grey; the desks are grey; the filing cabinets are grey; the walls are white; the only actual colour to relieve the situation in the entire building is in the office chairs. Since the upholstery on the chairs is not visible for most of the working day, as people are sitting on them, it is almost irrelevant, but it is a very warm, vivid, autumnal, tomato red. Whilst the inclusion of some red in the scheme is very sound, indeed essential to the balance, it should have been a cool crimson or cherry to support the cool grey; getting the tone so wrong only serves to negate the Winter tones everywhere else, and emphasize the cold negativity of the grey.

The colours in the building exactly reflect the attitude of the company – they like to present a warm, friendly face to the public (the pinky tones of the marble in reception), but the reality is much more neutral and uncommitted. The truth is, no matter how welcome you may feel as you approach this firm, the whole world inside it is grey so, once you are in, you will not be encouraged to grow and flourish, but constantly suppressed. Even if you arrive at work in the morning filled with enthusiasm and life, hours spent in a completely grey world will tell your system that you should draw in and contract as much as possible. You will feel drained by the end of the day.

One young accountant of my acquaintance worked at this firm for the first six years of his career and confirmed this. He was reasonably happy there, although slightly frustrated by the negative attitudes of the partners. He was aware that it was not a particularly happy company, but as a very lowly trainee he did not attach much importance to that – just ensured that his social life compensated for it. But when he left, he joined a smaller, more friendly company, whose partners saw him as an individual, with talents which should be encouraged to develop.

It was only then that he realized how suppressive the atmosphere had been in the previous job. He blossomed and rapidly reached senior management level. The decor throughout his new firm's offices is light peachy tones, with wooden desks and a carpet which he describes as 'rosy brick'. In fact, he finds that the emphasis in this company errs on the side of friendliness to the detriment of the work; he has to exercise considerable discipline. The absence of short-wavelength colours in the office could

have warned him that this would be the case. Some warm blue should be introduced.

The other example is the bill office in one of our most eminent five-star hotels. It used to be painted regularly in an attractive yellow, beautifully maintained – but only in the small rectangular space which was visible to the guests as they stood at the cashier's desk, paying their bills! The rest of the room was quite Dickensian; its dingy paintwork had not been renewed for so long that it was impossible to identify the colour. I have no idea how it looks today, but at that time – thirty or so years ago – staff morale was obviously not a major priority with the General Manager.

Once the tonal family, or season, has been established, which hues are appropriate for which workplaces?

OFFICES

The vast majority of office space is dedicated to cerebral activity and administrative, possibly repetitive, work. As a general rule of thumb, this applies if there are no drawing boards in there, and the staff tend to stay in all day. We shall examine exceptions to this – design offices and sales offices – in a moment.

As I have reiterated over and over again in this book, balance is as important as colour choice. In case the above example has put you off the idea of ever using grey in the office, let me assure you it can work quite well, in the right balance, with the right tones to harmonize it positively. You must always be aware, however, of the danger of overdoing grey and creating a negative atmosphere, reminiscent of the natural world during hibernation.

One of the key questions to examine is the nature of the business. Is the work stressful, or potentially very oppressive? Generally speaking, how do the people get on? Are there many people in the room? Is it a noisy office in terms of pure sound – telephones constantly ringing, machinery functioning, people inevitably having to consult each other about things?

If the office is dedicated to work which must be accurate – accountancy, insurance, banking, scientific research – or if you need to encourage people to concentrate calmly on their own work, the appropriate tone of blue is the best colour, every time – whichever season. Again, do not overdo it; whilst it will work well as the predominant colour in the scheme, it will still need to be relieved by some friendly yellows or pinks, or a touch of red, for the psychological balance. Perhaps cream walls and paintwork and a rich blue carpet would be a good basis. In this case, you would be advised to feature blue in any pictures you might hang, or find some way to echo the tone of the carpet at a higher physical level, even if only on the desks.

The reason for this is that colour on perpendicular planes is always more influential than on horizontal planes, and colour below knee level, or more than a couple of feet above the head, has less effect than colour surrounding your body; the most powerful influence is that at about eye level. For this reason, you may prefer to have light blue walls, in which case the carpet could be grey and the balancing warmth would have to come from upholstery or curtains.

In the personnel department, blue would still work, but green would probably be better, as it is so balanced. Weighing up all the pros and cons of issues surrounding the staff – recruitment, welfare, redundancy, wage bargaining etc. – would be greatly assisted by green. Nevertheless, you can afford to be a little more imaginative in there if you wish, because the nature of that department's work contains more variety than that of the accounts department. Peach, soft apricot or even some yellows could feature, and would go some way to dispel any possible perceptions of the personnel department being unnecessarily bureaucratic.

The sales team will not spend as much time in their office as everyone else, unless they are concerned with tele-sales, but either way they need the right kind of psychological support, perhaps even more than most. Do not create a heavy, dark atmosphere: they need to maintain a sense of optimism and a lift of spirits to keep them in the right frame of mind for the often demoralizing job of selling. Yellow is a brilliant choice of colour for this situation.

In the design department, balance becomes even more crucial; here an optimistic, creative mood should prevail, while designers must also be encouraged to focus accurately on the most effective way to achieve their objectives – alternative approaches are always possible in design, and clear thought is required.

It may be that the shape and lines of the drawing boards lead naturally to decorating the studio in Winter colours. White walls are good in this context, as they maximize the light, and do not create any particular colour bias in the room, but be careful that you do not make the environment too cold and clinical. It could also be good to use creative, optimistic light yellow. Generally speaking, it is advisable to avoid very strong colours in any design studio; often the work itself, apart from the drawing boards, is colourful anyway. It is certainly essential to avoid dark, suppressive colours.

The other element to take into account is the dominance of computers, word processors and other technology to be found in every office. Although some manufacturers are beginning to take a more adventurous view, for the moment most of the equipment comes in grey, or possibly stone beige. In themselves, if there are a lot of them, these items create a specific atmosphere, which you will need to counterbalance with some softening in the decor colours. Remember to consider, too, what happens when they are switched on – are they colourful, or constantly moving? This can be a strain.

SHOPS

We shall be looking in more depth at the whole area of retail design in Part Four, but it is worth a quick mention in this section from the point of view of the potential employee. As you will read in more detail later, I have worked on colour schemes for a number of shops, and in my experience much attention is always given to the best colours to use from the point of view of attracting customers in and encouraging them to buy. Until I point out to people that, essential as it is to accommodate the customers, they are only visiting, whilst the staff spend their entire working day there, it does not occur to shop owners what a vital effect the colour scheme can have on staff morale. Uniforms, too, tare always considered in terms of how they will look to potential customers and what image they will project about the company – never how the staff themselves will feel wearing them. We shall be looking more closely at the question of uniforms in the next chapter.

It is not difficult to see whether the needs of staff and customers in a shop have been properly taken into account if, as before, you focus on

A GLIMPSE OF
ASPIRATIONAL GLAMOUR
AT BERGDORF
GOODMAN IN NEW
YORK.

THE HUGE PROPORTIONS
AND COLD STEEL OF ALL
THIS MACHINERY ARE
SOFTENED BY THE WARM
LIGHTING AND GENTLE
TONE OF GREEN.

the basic proposition: what are they selling? Consider the Body Shop: their warm, autumnal green creates exactly the right atmosphere to turn the mind towards the earth and the environment, and tells you precisely what they are about – a reflection of the company's founder, Autumn-linked Anita Roddick.

If you are considering working in a shop, ask yourself what kind of atmosphere you find supportive. Is the merchandise something that you yourself would appreciate? Is the whole concept aimed predominantly at the young, in which case it will probably be staffed with young people, or is the emphasis on older people? How would you fit in?

Again, the merchandise will tell you that – a shop selling toys is obviously youth-oriented, and anyone going into that shop will go into the psychological mode of youth, fun and playtime, whilst a shop selling, say, antiquarian books will have a completely different atmosphere of timeless values, and probably be rather hushed. If either of these extremes is overdone, you run the risk of feeling either strained or drained if you are there all day. It is very important to ensure that the atmosphere is supportive to all concerned. Balance again.

One common approach to colour choices in shops is to keep the colours very neutral, since retailers do not wish to overshadow the merchandise. Often the only other colour comes from signage and point of sale material.

The best advice I can give you, if you are intending to work in a shop, is to go and stand in it for a while (you can pretend to be taking a great interest in the merchandise) and consciously try to absorb the atmosphere. Look at the colours – are they creating a warm, friendly, but not excessively stimulating mood? Or do you, after ten minutes or so, begin to develop a headache? Are they perhaps dreary and downbeat – might you begin to find yourself feeling rather negative if you had to work there? The best service that this book can provide for its reader is to heighten awareness of these questions, and get you to put more thought into them before you commit yourself to a career, or a career move.

INDUSTRIAL PREMISES

On the factory floor, colours are often governed by statutory regulations. Health and safety codes decree certain colours – traditionally green (reassurance) for first aid, yellow alone for caution, and combined with black to indicate hazardous chemicals. It used to be red for fire-fighting equipment, but these days fire-fighting codes are much more sophisticated: in Britain red indicates a water extinguisher, cream, green, blue and black extinguishers contain foam, halon, dry powder and carbon dioxide respectively, and safety officers in any commercial or industrial premises are trained by the fire brigade to know which appliance to use, depending on the type of fire.

The only problem now is that, after all the training effort, it has been decreed that the colours must be brought into line with codes devised in

Brussels for the whole European Union. Already we occasionally see chrome fire extinguishers, which I am told will eventually replace black; what is a little worrying is the danger of confusion in the meantime

Factory owners can perhaps be forgiven, when faced with the challenge of practical considerations, health and safety and compliance with so many bylaws, rules and regulations, if they feel that the psychology of colour is not for them. In fact, they are probably the ones who could benefit more than most from it. The work on the shop floor is essentially repetitive and can be stressful, industrial relations are fraught with potential tension. A misguided attempt to 'brighten the place up' by painting the walls in hectic colours does demonstrate that somebody cares and is making an effort, but it can misfire badly and be seriously counter-productive.

This is one context in which the seasonal decision is probably more relevant than the choice of hue. The premises are usually large, often have no natural daylight and are equipped with heavy machinery. Whether you choose green, yellow, blue or red derivative colours, I would always recommend Spring tones in this context, to lighten the atmosphere, both physically and psychologically. Clear blue, leaf green, daffodil yellow might not be the first choice for such a macho environment, but you may be surprised at how well these typical Spring tones work.

The method of increasing productivity attributed to Faber Birren in America many years ago strikes me as something of an abdication: it is said that, when commissioned to address the problem of productivity levels dropping because staff spent so much time in the rest rooms, instead of devising a supportive and positive colour scheme for the shop floor, he recommended the most negative colour he could find – a nauseating yellowish green – for the rest rooms. Nobody, but nobody, could face going in there other than as a matter of unavoidable necessity, and certainly no one was tempted to linger. The policy deserves top marks for lateral thinking, but has little else to recommend it in my opinion.

Finally, the question of lighting in the workplace is absolutely crucial to the health of the workforce. Sadly, it is often the case that it is only considered from the point of view of clear visibility, but the quality of the lighting and its effect on the colours is every bit as important. There are many different types of lighting; it is a very complex subject and not part of my remit, but I have the utmost respect for lighting experts, and always prefer to work with them wherever possible.

CHAPTER FIFTEEN

Uniforms

I f you have a job requiring you to wear a uniform – whether literally, or in the sense of an accepted dress code – it is worth bearing in mind that, whether it looks good on you or not, it can work to your advantage. If, for example, you are an inexperienced young police officer on the beat for the first time, it must be reassuring to know that you are already vested with authority, just by the clothes you are wearing. The uniform of a police officer and those of fire-fighters, paramedics, nurses, AA and RAC patrols, airline personnel, are very specific and distinctive, for practical reasons. People rely on them at the most basic level and they need to be instantly recognizable; their uniforms should not be too varied.

From the wearer's point of view, if you have completed a demanding training course and are entitled to wear a uniform that tells the world of your achievement, it is in itself a source of pride, and gives you a boost which is highly motivating. For instance, the traditional cap and gown worn by academics does not often suit anyone, in either colour or style, but the new graduate going up on to the dais to receive a degree feels a million dollars in it. (I notice, whenever I attend a graduation, that the graduates do not take off the gowns after the ceremony is over, but tend to sweep around the campus, posing delightedly for the rest of the day.) Older academics often rely on cap and gown to increase the sense of their authority.

There are many jobs in which it is inappropriate to assert individual personalities. One example of this is the traditional wearing of black by classical musicians, who must meld their individuality into the overall harmony of the music; somehow, a multi-coloured symphony orchestra would not work well; it would alter the whole atmosphere and distract attention from the music. It has been tried, but it is only a matter of time before the idea is quietly dropped and the musicians revert to traditional black. Of course, the tradition also serves to emphasize the contrasting bright colours worn by the soloists. If a musician who chafes against the restrictions and wants to be more creative in her dressing for a performance can understand the reasoning behind it, it is easier to accept.

UNIFORMS DON'T HAVE TO BE IDENTICAL

Nevertheless, apart from the very specific disciplines described above, in which the uniform has an independent character of its own, the wearer should not be completely ignored. Ideally some way should be found to permit an element of choice; this is usually achieved by giving people a choice of, say trousers or skirts for women, or differently designed shirts,

IT IS REASSURING FOR
YOUNG POLICE OFFICERS
ON THE BEAT TO KNOW
THAT THE UNIFORM IS
AUTHORITATIVE IN ITSELF.

different ties or scarves. Uniforms are rarely designed with a colour choice, as this is seen as defeating the object of having a uniform at all.

One of the most interesting projects I ever witnessed was when my teacher in California was commissioned to design the uniforms for staff at a bank. The corporate colours and the interior decor of the branches were fairly neutral, so she was not too restricted. The brief included some market research results indicating that the bank's public image was falling down on the perception of friendliness and approachability, so longer wavelength colours – ideally red – were required. At the same time, the bank was keen to protect its place in the public's perception as authoritative and reliable, which would suggest dark blue. We considered the physical combination of these values – red and blue make purple, so something in the violet family, leaning towards the red element, might have worked. Violet, however, has specific properties of its own and is very short wavelength.

The answer came to us both simultaneously, with no conscious thought process – burgundy. Burgundy, otherwise known as maroon, ruby, claret or garnet, is dark red, so it contains the friendly values of red, but is invested with seriousness and dignity by the addition of black (not at all the same process as using black itself in contrast). There are versions of it very close to the borderlines between all the seasons.

For reasons of budget and practicality, it would not have been sensible to suggest producing four different versions, but it was agreed that there should be a 'warm' version, with a hint of golden undertones, and a 'cool' version, containing a touch of blue, nearer to the colour that you would

TURQUOISE IS A GOOD
COLOUR FOR UNIFORMS —
STRICTLY SPEAKING A
SPRING TONE, IT IS
USEFUL FOR RECONCILING
DIFFERENCES BETWEEN
THE SEASONAL PALETTES.
FOR BARCLAY'S BANK,
OF COURSE, IT HAS THE
ADDED ADVANTAGE OF
REFLECTING THE
CORPORATE COLOURS.

see if you held a glass of burgundy up to the light. The difference between them was virtually indistinguishable to the eye of the casual observer, but we found that when they were invited to choose, all the staff had a definite preference. We knew, of course, that this was an indication of their own season, but we did not need to complicate things by going into lengthy explanations; we were able to rely on each individual's instincts to lead him or her in the right direction. We also had two tones for the shirts – a creamy ivory to go with the warm-toned jackets and a cool oyster white for the others.

It worked very well. Nobody who walked into the bank was ever heard to observe that there were two versions of the uniform; the staff did not usually stand side by side, but when they did, the colours were so close to each other that one might have assumed it was just a different dye batch. In terms of the effect on the wearer, and the ongoing psychological support of a sympathetic shade, the difference was tremendous.

This was a complex project, and you would need to be very sure of your knowledge of colour to take that approach. There are other ways: you can choose a version of one of the three Spring colours I mentioned in Part One as being so balanced as to be almost acceptable in all four seasons – turquoise, peach or cream (off white), although the latter two are rather too light to be practical. Alternatively, if your company has a distinctive corporate colour you can echo that, on the basis that most of your employees must have been attracted to that colour at some stage, as they are working for you now.

It saddens me to see how often people opt out of using any imagination or giving real thought to the whole concept of uniforms. Time and time again we see the same boring thing – grey or navy, cold and suppressive. The only application I can think of where this approach is entirely appropriate is in the black, grey or navy clothes worn by priests and nuns in the Catholic Church, where the aim is to help suppress the more carnal aspects of their nature. This makes a very interesting contrast to the glorious colours the Church uses throughout the year in its services, when the aim is to inspire the congregation. Obviously, other Christian Churches use colour in similar ways, but it works particularly well for the Catholics with their rule of celibacy.

The majority of oriental people look wonderful, but only about one in ten of the population in the Western world looks and feels really good, in dark navy. For the rest, it drains the face and drags you down. The idea of using it for a uniform, presumably, is to promote a serious, professional image, but it is perfectly possible to achieve that with warmer tones such as cobalt blue, teal blue, camel, brown, burgundy, forest green or aubergine.

People seem to think it does not matter, but to suppress the majority of the workforce and dress them drearily is to miss the golden opportunity that uniforms afford. If you know what you are doing, and dress the staff in clothes which improve their self-image and at the same time give the clientèle a good impression, you will materially affect your business to a far greater degree than most people realize. There is no doubt that people dressed in clothes which make them feel good about themselves perform to a much higher standard; productivity will rise and stress levels reduce.

If you are considering going to work for a company, the colour of the uniform will give you an idea of how the management really sees its staff. I find myself feeling slightly irritated when I hear people referring to the most boring and dreary uniforms as 'smart', as in, 'We'll put them all in smart suits,' when they mean, 'We don't know what to put them in, so let's play safe. As long as we prevent them from wearing jeans to work, that is all right.'

'UNOFFICIAL' UNIFORMS

Whilst many disciplines do not have a uniform, accepted dress codes apply with almost as much rigidity as if they did. Traders making a name for themselves in the City of London, or any other financial centre, would get nowhere if they turned up for work in anything but the snappy suit (male or female) and, for the men, striped shirt, dramatic tie and braces. Throughout the 1980s, removing the jacket was not just a matter of temperature; it was making a fashion statement which required absolutely that fancy braces – preferably red – were worn.

Senior and middle management everywhere wear suits in the office. A woman might get away with a dress, but only if she has a jacket elegantly draped over the back of her chair. People who can generally be described as 'creatives' make a point of not wearing suits. In an advertising agency or design consultancy you can recognize the account handlers – those who act as liaison between creative personnel and clients – by the fact that they are the only people who wear suits, in line with the clients.

I am obviously not able to see inside the heads of designers as they make their dress decisions in the morning, but I wonder if they are aware of how drearily most of them dress, most of the time? It is almost a uniform with them to live and die in dark, suppressive colours, more often than not black, or possibly grey.

The people who have made the break from traditional attitudes towards dress are the new wave of computer experts. IBM was always known for its rigid insistence that all its executives wore dark blue suits, white shirts and dark red, plain ties, and played everything 'the company way', but now the 'Young Turks' of Silicon Valley and around the world have adopted a typically Californian approach, and dress as informally as anyone going to a barbecue or a picnic. People are encouraged to express themselves more freely, and what a person wears is considered infinitely less important than what he is or how she thinks, and the philosophy is spreading.

I am not certain that this policy is absolutely accurate every time. People still register what a person is wearing and, as we know, unconsciously respond strongly to the colours. Most of us recognize this and are often quite grateful to be able to retreat behind a dress code which does not require too much overt commitment to our own self-expression. Some people do prefer some external guidance on what is appropriate.

In America, the practice of designating Friday as an informal dress day, known as Dress Down Day, is spreading, and many people welcome the idea of getting into the weekend mode slightly ahead of time. It is said that, rather than encouraging slackness, it is found to be increasing productivity. This appears to support the philosophy of those who would do away with all uniforms and dress codes completely. My guess is that, once that had been achieved and the pressure to conform removed, people would gradually drift back to the old ways, of their own accord.

Antipathy towards the concept of wearing a uniform often harks back to adolescent rebellion, and indeed it is often a fact that school uniforms do little, if anything, for the wearer. If you really resent your professional dress code, and feel that it does not suit you, perhaps you should seriously consider whether you are in the right job? Dress codes and uniforms clearly reflect underlying attitudes which it would benefit you to consider at the outset.

PART FIVE

COLOUR IN COMMERCE

CHAPTER SIXTEEN

The Chairman's Wife

One day, driving through London, I approached the roundabout at Elephant and Castle, a major junction, where the shopping centre had been under wraps for several months, with scaffolding and tarpaulin obscuring it from view. I almost crashed my car, so amazed was I at the sight that met my eyes. The covers had gone, and the refurbishment was revealed for all the world to see. The whole of the shell of the shopping centre was vivid bubble-gum pink! This large edifice, dominating the roundabout, had literally become a traffic hazard overnight. The signage of the various shops in the centre conspired to add to the problem – Tesco, with its vivid red logo, being the worst. How could this be allowed? What were the designers and architects on? Did someone actually think that this would attract people into the centre? Was it seen as a potential improvement for the urban landscape?

I tracked down the people concerned and was advised that:

a) in general, planning permission is not required for colour on public buildings, unless they are listed, and

b) in the case of the 'pink elephant', people either loved it or loathed it.

The main objective, as I understand it, was to create a dramatic improvement on the drabness of the building that had been there before. Well, it was certainly dramatic!

I am constantly amazed at the lack of awareness of colour amongst those who really should know better. People who are working with colour every day – architects, designers, printers, marketing executives, employees of cosmetics companies – do not appear to realize how potent an influence it is, and are not prepared to devote time and study to the proper understanding of it, and to developing an attitude bordering on reverence for its wonder. They apparently prefer to trivialize and misuse it, with no respect for its truth, its beauty and its power – or worse, to relegate it to the completely incidental; if this is how they feel, I wonder why they choose a career in which colour plays such a pivotal role? They would be better advised to leave colour alone.

My first attempts to interest the design world in my work were often disregarded. It was not that people were hostile – more dismissive. They just kept saying, 'Yes. Yes. We know' and I felt as if I were trying to shout through a mouthful of cotton wool. It was obvious to anyone looking around at the misuse of colour in public buildings, at the madness of supermarket shelves, signage, packaging, TV advertising – designer wit gone mad – that they did *not* know.

Sometimes I would be asked to address groups of designers, who would come up to me afterwards, expressing great interest, indeed excitement, in what I was telling them:

'This is really fascinating – food for thought!'

Then they would go right on doing things the same old way, apparently making no connection between thought and action. It was as if it had nothing to do with them and their work. Indeed, although considerable progress has been made, widespread understanding of colour still has a long way to go.

COLOUR IN COMMERCIAL DESIGN

The implications of using colour psychology across the commercial world to influence people's unconscious responses and purchasing decisions are enormous, and cover packaging, interiors, advertising and promotional material of all kinds.

At this point, it is perhaps a good idea to explain the difference between the public perception of the concept of 'design' and the way the design industry sees itself (I am not referring to fashion design in this context). The average person in the street, asked to define the word 'design', tends to do so in terms of function before aesthetic pleasure. When we talk of great design classics we usually consider such memorable examples as the Mini or the Volkswagen Beetle, the Bauhaus, Wranglers and, today, the work of Philippe Starck. If someone says a thing is well designed, we usually take that to mean that it works well.

Since the 1960s, however, all that has changed. The concept of design was broadened by the work of people like Terence Conran in Britain and Frenchman Raymond Loewy in America, to embrace aesthetic considerations in everyday commerce. These pioneers buried once and for all the myth that aesthetic excellence costs too much for the masses, and that designers are artists paid by the very rich to indulge themselves. People began to recognize that design is of fundamental importance, and that professional designers have a valuable contribution to make in virtually every area of our lives.

In the 1990s, whilst every manufacturing company still has its team of product designers, and indeed there are as many product designers as ever, pure function often falls into the remit of the ergonomists. The traditional product designers and interior designers have been joined by a raft of specialists, under the umbrella term 'graphic designers', producing such things as packaging and brochures, once the province of commercial artists and printers. It is very big business, and it has all expanded and developed so fast, even the designers themselves are not quite sure what they are. Every so often arguments break out in the design press about whether it is an industry or a profession. What is clear is that literally millions are spent each year on design – but as much by the marketing department as by the production department.

THE 'OLD GUARD'
CLASSIC QUALITY OF THE
ROLLS-ROYCE...

CORPORATE IMAGES

As you become more familiar with the links between patterns of colour and patterns of human behaviour, the potential for applying the principles of colour psychology and the seasonal classifications of personality types to any entity become obvious. A company has its corporate culture, its essential nature, its personality, its public image, just as a person has these facets individually. People – i.e. that company's potential clients – respond on a personal level to the company in just the same way as they respond to anything else they encounter.

It is common these days for marketing people to establish the nature of any proposition, be it a new product, a piece of packaging or a company's whole corporate identity, in terms of its personality. At the first briefing, someone will say something like,

'If this company (pack, product) were a car, what kind of car would it be? A Ford Sierra? A BMW? A Porsche or a Rolls-Royce?'

Each of these cars possesses perceived characteristics way beyond reality, and everyone recognizes the difference between, say, the young and slightly flashy image of a Porsche and the classic quality of a Rolls-Royce. A Ford Sierra conjures up another personality and a BMW is different again. These perceptions have nothing to do with the price of the product.

...CONTRASTS WITH THE YOUNGER IMAGE OF A PORSCHE. THE SOBER BLUE AND METALLIC SILVER REINFORCE OUR INSTINCTIVE RESPONSES.

THE ELEPHANT AND CASTLE SHOPPING CENTRE IN LONDON — 'A DRAMATIC IMPROVEMENT ON THE DREARINESS OF THE BUILDING BEFORE'.

The process of deciding on colours in commercial design is an interest-ing one; the decision is essentially still made on the basis of rank. No mat-ter how much expertise is developed, and investment made in designers and expensive computers to aid the process, the 'Chairman's Wife' syn-drome is still alive and well. Although it can be very frustrating for more junior personnel, I nevertheless do not dismiss out of hand the instinct of the most senior person involved in a project. He or she probably under-stands their own business better than I do.

When I am confronted by a strongly held opinion about the best colour to use, it is vital to ascertain whether this certainty derives from a clear vision, or reflects a personal problem. Very often a senior executive will cling to a colour in the absence of any other tangible means of asserting control over a project. Since colour response is still seen as a matter of subjective opinion, it is an area that can legitimately be asserted by some-one with no design training. Time and time again I am told in a design brief that the corporate colours are sacrosanct, and must not be changed.

More often than not, if those have been the corporate colours for more than ten years or so, they are entirely appropriate anyway; if they were not working, the fact would have been instinctively recognized, and the colours would have been changed. In this case my job is to make the colours work *better*. Often the core colour is being compromised by another colour with it, so it is not necessary to change the core colour itself, but to introduce colours which will support and enhance it, bring it more up to date – whatever is required.

One striking example of this is the famous Heinz Baked Beans blue. There are many theories about why this has been so spectacularly successful, and I will add my own: blue in general, and a blue veering towards turquoise in particular, is a very popular colour worldwide, as we have already noted. The Heinz Beans blue originally presented a departure from the usual 'food' colours, which increased its initial impact, and – crucially – it is an autumnal tone, so it has inherent properties of rich abundance and solid substance – all very good news for a staple food.

I have heard it said that the precise blue is complementary to the colour of the product, and indeed it is, but I find that rather tenuous, as one does not see them together; that fact would only come into its own in promot-ing the product if the customer could be persuaded to stare at the tin for thirty seconds and then shut his eyes, enabling the after image to present an optical illusion of seeing the contents of the tin.

At the time of writing, the design of the Heinz Baked Beans label is considerably compromising the famous blue, because the black keystone device and white lettering draw all the warmth and power from the blue, making it look slightly jaded and old-fashioned (the negative perception of positive tried and true familiarity). Of course there is no argument that it is a wonderfully successful piece of branding, but equally there is no doubt that the power of the brand could be even further increased if the rest of the colours were harmonized so that they supported and enhanced the core blue.

Realistically, it has to be said that the key to long-term success of any corporate colour lies in the quality of actual performance. In the case of Heinz Beans, that blue would not have gone into the annals of marketing history if the product were no good. The psychology of colour – and indeed any aspect of presentational (as opposed to functional) design – will only sell a product once. Furthermore, if the packaging design or the corporate identity creates expectations which are unrealistic, it will back-fire seriously. For this reason, it is important to understand very clearly what precisely you are selling, and then concentrate on presenting its most attractive face – rather than creating an expectation of a completely differ-ent product or service.

COLOUR SYMBOLISM

If the corporate colour is not communicating the most positive aspects of the company, or the brand, it has been my experience that this fact always becomes clear to everyone involved as the project develops and under-standing of colour psychology deepens. Just as with individual people, it is not part of my brief to tell anyone what colours to use, but to advise them of the psychological implications, so that they can make their own informed, rational decisions.

Nobody in his right mind would suggest that a well-established and familiar corporate colour should be changed. Such icons as Cadbury's pur-ple, Coca Cola's red and white, McDonald's golden arches on red work well because somewhere along the way, many years ago, someone – pos-sibly the Chairman's Wife – chose exactly the right colours to capture the essence of the proposition and it worked. Eventually another factor entered the equation, that of familiarity. In terms of colour psychology – the unconscious effects – Cadbury's pure violet, for example, originally communicated the ultimate in fine quality and uncompromising standards, but those perceptions were long ago overtaken by the conscious associa-tions created, by its continued use, in the mind of the general public between that particular purple and chocolate – colour symbolism.

Even that powerful colour can be compromised, however, by the other colours on the pack. It needs to be supported every time it is used.

I understand that one of Cadbury's more successful launches, quite exceeding expectation, was their Twirl bar. Could it be a coincidence that the lettering on that pack is a powerful Winter yellow, evoking excitement and lively optimism – and exactly complementary to the Cadbury's violet? I don't think so.

More recently the company has had a spectacular success with the launch of another new bar, Time Out. This time a pure Group IV red has been used for the lettering, outlined with that Winter yellow again. In each case the variant colours are working with the core colour, rather than against it.

A commercial arena which demonstrates particularly effectively how corporate colours affect public perception is that of oil companies and their petrol stations. Each of the major players, all of whom have been lodged in our consciousness for as long as the motor car, has a very specific place in the public scheme of things. I was asked to write an analysis of the public image of three major companies – Texaco, Shell and BP – based solely on their use of colour.

This document described how Texaco's black and pure red with white, supported by the sharp angles of the star logo, are Group IV – Winter – and communicate efficiency and technical excellence, but must be applied carefully to skirt around the danger of red's negative face – aggression – combining with black's negativity – menace. They are essentially masculine, and I would anticipate that this is where the car enthusiast, or the biker, would go.

Shell, with its pecten logo hardly changed in over a century, and its warm Group III (Autumn) yellow and red, represents tried and trusted traditional values; warm and friendly, but not scoring very highly in terms of advanced technology and modernity. With no shorter wavelength, or serious, colours, it is slightly unbalanced.

BP, on the other hand, who might have been thought to be unbalanced in the amount of green they used for their revamp, chose the colour of balance, so it works. Combined with the clear yellow, it presents a Spring colour scheme which conveys a sense of youth, a new generation, optimism and warm friendliness – although perhaps not as authoritative as it might be. (I was not asked to analyse Esso, but they use the softer end of the Winter palette, and round shapes, so they present a picture of friendliness combined with forward thinking.) I was subsequently given sight of the findings of a major market research study, which confirmed exactly what I had observed.

Any motorist will agree that we all have our own favourite and will sometimes go out of our way to fill up at one of their stations. Think about it – is the lone female motorist, unexpectedly short of petrol on a quiet road late at night, going to be attracted to the strong masculine efficiency, with a possible hint of menace, of Texaco, or the friendly reliability of Shell? Which petrol station does the mechanically minded person seek out? Do you regard BP predominantly with awe and respect, or with affection? When we consider that all the petrol stations are essentially selling exactly the same product, the mythology that has grown around the perceived differences between them is very interesting.

UNDERSTANDING YOUR PRODUCT

The first question that people ask about packaging or interior design in public places is, 'What about the unpredictable elements of personal preference? You can't please all of the people all of the time.'

In many ways, colour in commerce works exactly the same way as in personal presentation. If you take the trouble to understand the essential nature of the commercial proposition and present it in its most appropriate colours – the tonal family which most supports and enhances its positive aspects – you give people the opportunity to identify clearly what it is, and this recognition engenders a sense of security which will encourage them to do business with you.

I am in fact reiterating what I have already said about personal palettes – if you try to present yourself in terms of what you think 'they' (whoever 'they' may be) think you should be about, you are on a hiding to nothing. Whilst it is vital for a marketer to understand the market, it is also essential to attach the same importance to understanding the product, so that a cohesive, recognizable offer is presented, which is not losing its own identity in a vain attempt to be all things to all people.

So often, marketers and designers are so busy trying to combine every possible virtue that they think their offer should encompass that they end up sending out a jumble of contradictory messages which the potential purchaser frankly has neither the time nor the interest to try and unravel. It takes the average customer approximately fifteen seconds to respond, for example, to an item on a supermarket shelf, and make the purchasing decision.

Millions of pounds are spent on the development of new products – 'NPD' – but the percentage of new products which never make it is a staggering 80 per cent. The reasons for this are complex, but much of this failure derives from ill-considered relationships among the quality of the product, the target market and the presentation; it is simply not thought through properly. Marketers so often look in any direction but that of the inherent properties of their product for inspiration.

―――――――――――― ## THE 'LANGUAGE OF THE SECTOR' ――――――――――――

Packaging designers often cling to the notion of 'the language of the sector' without realizing that the average shopper is oblivious of it. I remember some years ago addressing a conference attended by Marketing Directors from a wide variety of major companies, and getting myself into considerable grief with the Marketing Director of one of the big four supermarket chains in Britain, when I made this observation. He dismissed out of hand the possibility that washing powder, for example, could be packaged in anything but white and strong primary – almost day-glo – colours, or that pet-food cans could be labelled in anything but red for beef, yellow for chicken, etc.

'The public read the colour signals absolutely!' he declared.

This is true, but the colour signals are rarely communicated absolutely. What is communicated is a jumble of colour symbolism, which will be instantly overridden every time by the unconscious power of accurately applied colour psychology.

It was shortly after this conference that my view was borne out by a brilliant example of a successful new product launch – the washing powder Radion. At first glance, it would seem to be madness to present a new washing powder in a bright orange and blue pack. It flew in the face of traditional symbolism and the language of the sector, of associations with the concept of 'whiter than white'.

What the marketers of Radion understood was that they were not just selling whiteness. They were selling efficiency and strength above and beyond anything hitherto experienced. Orange is a strong, physical colour, which focuses on abundance, and blue conveys reliable, well-researched efficiency. Remember, too, that blue and orange are complementary colours, and therefore mutually intensify. All the tones on the pack were in the Winter family – Persian orange, Reflex blue, a little white and touches of Winter lime green – so the message of that particular combination was underpinned by unconscious perceptions of the Winter characteristics of leadership, strength and uncompromising standards. Radion did not ask us to like it – there was no attempt to engender affection for the brand – this was state-of-the-art, and the unconscious expectation created by these colours was that, even if we did not particularly like it, it would get the job done for us, better than it had ever been done before.

It worked. In no time, Radion was snapping at the heels of dear old Persil, its stablemate (whose Autumn green and red tones, though compromised by the white background, have always communicated a balance of traditional values and friendliness – again, please note, complementary colours) and threatening the latter's long-held dominance of the market.

Another example of the myth of the 'language of the sector' was the launch of Vidal Sassoon's Wash'n'Go shampoo/conditioner. Everyone thought the company had taken leave of its senses when light, bright, Spring aqua-green was proposed for the bottle. Even the designers themselves were very doubtful, and concerned that it was not an appropriate shampoo packaging colour. The client's view prevailed, however, and it was only a matter of six months from its launch that the brand was the market leader.

I suggest that the reason it worked so well was that, since it was not a traditional shampoo, but a new concept, packaging it in a colour that was new to shampoo served to emphasize that. Also, being a Group I (Spring) tone, the aqua-green communicated lightness and movement, entirely supportive of the concept, presented by the advertising, of youth and lively activity: 'Why spend more time in the shower than I need?'

I had a stand-up battle over the same question with a very gifted young designer who commissioned me to produce a palette for him. The product was a low-calorie bedtime drink. It was a new generation brand from an old-established company, and the essential proposition was all about youth and lightness, and about demonstrating that the old firm knew how to move with the times. It was to be promoted as a 'premium' brand – i.e. a luxury product. The corporate colour of the parent brand was a rich, autumnal dark blue, but that was not required to appear on the pack, so for the predominant colour I was able to recommend a nicely balanced, light turquoise blue from the Spring family. Blue is a soothing colour, and presenting this new product in a lighter, livelier Spring palette suggested that it was warm and friendly – the perceptions they wished to communicate were built in.

The danger of using Spring colours is that the positive youth and freshness of the colours might be converted into immaturity and be perceived as cheap and frivolous if they are negated or overpowered by being combined with colours from a different family. I included a light, warm gold in the palette to emphasize the luxury element.

The designer was delighted with the colours, and recognized that the light turquoise captured the proposition accurately. However, he decided that the language of the sector was paramount, and, instead of adopting the palette as a whole, he incorporated the Spring turquoise alone into a disparate colour selection (it could not be called a palette) of his own, based on the language of the sector. He added white, and exchanged the gold for silver stripes – the traditional indication of a low-calorie variant. His client's reaction was, 'It looks like a cheap, flashy 1950s car, complete with chrome trim!'

The designer had fallen between the two stools of traditional use of colour and colour psychology, which highlighted another important point: if a designer (or anyone else) decides to adopt the system of colour psychology, based on tonal groups as described in this book, it is no good unless the whole system is adopted for the project. Trying to incorporate one tone into a traditional colour scheme will not work, and may make matters worse – far better to stick to the traditional way.

The language of the sector is commercial design's exact equivalent to fashion in the context of personal presentation. If you take it to its natural conclusion, it becomes clear that the whole thing is a myth. If it were not, then every single similar product in the marketplace would be presented in exactly the same colours – which they demonstrably are not. But take it a step further – if they were, there would be little to distinguish one brand from another, so we might as well abandon the whole concept of sophisticated packaging design to promote sales. (This may not necessarily be a bad thing, but that is not the issue here.)

Sadly, this same myth is often used as an excuse for a clichéd, lazy approach to design. One cannot necessarily blame designers for their lack of original flair – whilst originality is deeply satisfying and creates the most impact, it inevitably carries risks – but it is depressing.

I have observed the whole process of design, and it is as if everyone approaches it with a strong sense of insecurity and mutual suspicion. The client expects the designer to be able to rationalize the design (again, translating right-brain activity into left-brain terms) in order to counter the suspicion that the latter is simply indulging himself – a suspicion which is naturally resented. The designer cannot simply address the proposition objectively, with a completely open mind, and allow his creative talents free rein, because his motivation is based on what he thinks the brand managers at the client company are going to like, rather than what is best for promoting the product. The brand managers in their turn are wondering if they will be able to sell the design on to their superiors, whatever their own response to it may be, and the Marketing Director knows that if the product bombs it will be her head on the block – she needs to have a sensible justification ready. Whilst there are training courses and degrees to be gained in the business of marketing, it remains a highly esoteric process, with many imponderables which are impossible to predict. The Chairman's Wife is as good a benchmark as any.

The truth is that often the designer has no idea why a design is right – he is acting on a well-developed instinct. I had a telephone call one day from a great chum of mine, who asked me if I could give him a rational explanation for a colour scheme he had devised (without my help), for one colour in which the client was now requesting reasons.

'I can't just tell her it felt right, can I!' he wailed.

He described the proposition in detail, and the colours he had used. I was easily able to explain to him the thinking process which had underpinned the design, even though much of it had been reached instinctively rather than consciously thought through, and I confirmed that the particular colour his client was questioning was right.

'Gosh,' he said. 'Is that why I did it? Aren't I clever!'

One of the reasons I did eventually break down the initial apathy towards my work was that, by presenting a written, objective rationale to explain the reasoning behind specific colour choices, I was able to remove much of the sort of insecurity I have just described. Everyone down the line was relieved of the necessity of expressing an opinion, however educated, upon which literally millions of pounds could hang.

In the early days it was rather nerve-wracking, but as my experience grew and predicted responses were more and more often confirmed in market research (sometimes verbatim), I felt less nervous about going out on a limb. The only times that things went wrong were on the few occasions when I allowed myself to be led away from the absolute principles of colour psychology, to try and accommodate strongly held opinions, or other considerations such as the language of the sector or the conscious associations of established colours.

It is very obvious that every single brand of product has its own, unique characteristics which cannot be exactly copied – although we do see a lot of 'me too!' design appearing after a particularly good new product launch. If those unique characteristics are accurately identified, then translated into colours which communicate the values of the brand, the product stands a much better chance of success. Having the courage of well thought-out convictions is as successful in the marketplace as it is in any other area of life.

CHAPTER SEVENTEEN

Neatly Packaged

We have established that a clear understanding of the product is essential to its successful marketing. Nevertheless it is an undisputed fact that clever packaging will manipulate the public perception of any product quite beyond reality. In the realm of women's cosmetics, for instance, countless impartial exercises in comparative analysis of various brands confirm that cheaper products are every bit as effective, and sometimes more so, as the most expensive; the truth is they are often identical, because there are a very small number of manufacturers, who produce cosmetics for several different companies. But women continue to be seduced by the luxury of expensive packaging – even to the point of feeling quite insecure about buying a cheap product. The shape, size, colour and style of a pack tune in very powerfully to your psyche, and push buttons you probably don't realize you have. Designers and marketers are very aware of this, and most of them have mastered a useful grasp of psychology.

THE 'PSYCHOLOGICAL MODE'

I referred earlier to the concept of psychological mode. In the world of advertising, marketing and sales promotion, markets used to be identified mainly by socio-economic groupings, based on the idea that purchasing decisions were purely a matter of money, and that people in certain types of job, within specific income brackets, would share a great number of characteristics and all tend to buy the same sort of goods, thus constituting a target market. In recent years, for a variety of reasons, the shortcomings of such a simplistic system of classification have become clear. Jung's personality types have formed the basis of newer groupings, which take account of the reality that rich people and poor people can share the same human traits, the same hopes and aspirations.

More recent still is the concept of mode analysis. This accepts that anyone might be attracted to any kind of product if it reflects the psychological mode he or she is in. For example, any person, be they prince or pauper, male or female, young or old, when considering a cold cure, feels the same; they are in the psychological mode of having a cold. Either they already have it, or they can feel it coming on and are imagining themselves when the symptoms are in full flow. Hence a pack with too much warmth (reds, pinks, etc.) in it will have associations with fever and inflammation and therefore less appeal than colours with inherent properties of light and clarity, which provide a lift of spirits and optimism (Group I, Spring). By the time that same person has gone from the chemist to the pet shop (or if they were in a supermarket to start with, gone to another aisle) to buy some cans of pet food, they are in a different mode altogether. They are now identifying with their pet, and picturing themselves in a happy relationship with the animal.

Pet food is an enormous sector of the market, and there is little doubt that the attitudes of dog owners and cat owners are very specific, but often quite different from each other. (If you have both, and love them equally, you are an animal lover, which is different again.) The appeal of a cat lies in its grace and beauty, its independence and the sense of it bestowing its affection on you and taking up residence with you only if you deserve it. Cats will attach themselves more to a home (territory) than to its occupants. It is virtually impossible to train a cat, because basically a cat is not remotely interested in your approval. We mere humans admire and rather aspire to feline sophistication. Dogs, on the other hand, love unconditionally, and attach themselves to people, with 'dogged' devotion. They like nothing better than to be out with you in the open, with plenty of space to run around and play, preferably with you, getting thoroughly muddy; they are eternally loyal. Dogs are not interested in their dignity (or yours).

Pedigree Petfoods created an enormous impact when they decided to present their whole range of Whiskas cat food in a vivid Group IV – Winter – purple. It was a bold move, but it worked because it caught the psychological mode of the cat owner (or the characteristics of the cat, if you like). They expanded their range, so an added bonus developed in the impact of a large block of strong colour on the shelves. The cans were impossible to miss. As is so often the case, however, when designers have hit upon exactly the right colour instinctively, they do not fully understand why it works and therefore cannot apply objective criteria to the question of variant colours – they put all kinds of colours on the pack to indicate the different flavours, etc., which often compromise the pure power of that purple.

A remarkable example of the power of colour in packaging is Smith & Nephew's brand of cosmetics called Simple. Simple products were packaged in natural white, with a strong eco-friendly earth-brown logo and lettering. The name Simple itself encompassed everything desirable about the brand, and it was very much in tune with the developing mood of people beginning to worry about so many environmental issues of pollution and excessive use of chemicals. It was a very successful brand. However, when Smith & Nephew decided to redesign the pack, and it was changed to a soft Group II (Summer) tone of green, with grey lettering, on the cool, slightly off-white background, the volume of sales immediately rose by a further dramatic 27 per cent. The company was, of course, delighted.

The simplistic interpretation of Smith & Nephew's experience was that the brown was not a good colour in itself, and when it was changed to green, the packaging worked better. This is not necessarily the case by any means. Again I stress that there is no such thing as a good or a bad colour – it is entirely a matter of how it is used. That green could equally easily be compromised and lose its effect. What caused the increase in appeal was the switch from a pack struggling to reconcile two colours which had no relationship with each other to an innately harmonious presentation; although there was rather too much of the brown on the original pack, it was appropriate to the offer, and could have been retained and made to work better, but combining it with cool white was negating it, making it appear heavy and unattractive.

White is a matter of pure habit – a white background is so common that we do not realize how negatively it can act on other colours, and rarely ascribe failure of a colour scheme to it. Changing the colour balance, removing the white and using that Group III (autumnal) brown with a palette from the light end of Autumn could have worked to continue the heritage of the brand and reinforce its perceived values of environmental awareness. The alternative approach, of removing it altogether and keeping the cool white, combined with tones which harmonized in Group II (Summer), communicated different, but equally positive values – the characteristics of green in a context of Summer attributes of fine quality, delicacy and gentleness. It worked brilliantly. The point about this example is that it serves to remind us that people do not respond to any one colour in isolation, but to the harmony, or otherwise, that exists in the relationship of all the colours.

Dark brown, used very differently, works very successfully for Vidal Sassoon's hair products. At the time of writing, they are in the process of redesigning their packaging – it will be interesting to see what happens.

In the late 1960s Scholl Consumer Products, founded by the late Dr Scholl and predominantly concerned with footcare, commissioned designers to redesign their packaging and presentation. It was decided that the distinctive yellow should go, and be replaced by white packaging. Although I was not personally involved in this – the story was told to me by a former employee of the company, who was – I can imagine the debate:

'White stands out and is a nice, hygienic colour – it will increase the impression of the product being medically effective.'

It was an almost complete disaster, and the yellow was rapidly reinstated. Yellow is potentially a very appropriate colour for footcare products, because it is the colour of lightness and optimism, easily encouraging a psychological mode of being light on your feet – even dancing! In the case of Dr Scholl, the particular yellow is a rich, autumnal tone, therefore creating the context of strength, and it is perfectly balanced by a harmonious dark blue from the same tonal group. It was also firmly established in the public mind as the colour for Scholl products, and had acquired a value of its own; removing it was a great mistake.

One company which understood this concept very clearly was Vax

THE AUTUMNAL GREEN ON THE BOWYERS PACK BRINGS THE RICHNESS OF THE COUNTRY INTO THE SUPERMARKET.

WALLS'S WINTER TONES EMPHASIZE QUALITY AND HIGH STANDARDS OF HYGIENE.

Appliances. I was idly watching TV some years ago and was suddenly riveted by a series of commercials, done in black and white or sepia, wherein the only colour was an orange, dancing around the screen. I had read in the marketing press that Vax had decided to invest its company's values and presentation in the colour orange. I wrote to the company and enquired if they had sought advice about the psychological implications of the colour orange before making this decision. The Marketing Director telephoned me the next day:

'Good grief!' she said. 'We have never even thought of the psychology of orange. When can you get here?'

I went to see them and explained about the properties of orange itself, and the importance of protecting its positive perceptions. The original product had been invented by the company's founder, Alan Brazier, a former dairy farmer whose inspiration for the design came from his milk churns, and it was a major success story. The product was orange and black, which created a strong impact for something new; whilst the orange (Group III – Autumn) was appropriate, with its perceptions of abundance, strength and warmth, the heavy use of black somewhat negated these values and gave it an industrial feel, which had to be overcome by any potential customer considering taking this rather large item into the home. There was no doubt that the machine would work, but it was not as attractive as it might be.

Vax were just expanding their range and developing new models, so my arrival was very timely. Even if I had needed to, which I did not, it would not have been helpful to the company at that point for me to criticize the orange, into which so much money and public commitment had already been invested; my job was to advise them of its precise psychological implications and provide them with a palette of colours to replace the black in supporting the core colour and making it work really positively every time. No matter what the core colour had been, even if it had not been particularly appropriate, this would still have been possible. Vax revisited issues of colour balance and reduced the amount of orange, whilst maintaining its chromatic intensity; their next model was rather less orange, with blue – complementary colours. It was very successful and the company continues to use that palette.

———— 'NO SUCH THING AS A GOOD OR BAD COLOUR' ————

The truth underlying all these examples emphasizes yet again that the question 'What is a good colour for...?' has no answer beyond 'It depends.' When people in commerce first hear about my work, they assume I must always use the same colours for, let us say, all insurance companies, or that there is only one ideal colour for the packaging of all products of a similar nature. To demonstrate what a fallacy this is, let us consider an example I worked on some years ago: the simple sausage.

The Walls range of sausages, bacon, etc., is extremely successful and for as long as I can remember Walls have packaged these products in navy blue, with red and white. The colours are Group IV – Winter – tones and, despite the received wisdom that food should never be packaged in blue because 'it is not a food colour', it is very effective. As we have seen, Winter colours in general communicate efficiency, hygiene and attention to detail, and dark blue is the ultimate expression of authority and reliability. This is entirely appropriate for the market leader, and the consumer is reassured that the family is unlikely to be poisoned by this product. The message contained in the pack is that Walls are quite simply the best.

I was asked to advise on colour for Bowyers, whose products are in direct competiton with the mighty Walls on the supermarket shelves. If we had just baldly considered the product, it would have been a very limited exercise – hardly worth doing. As it was, everyone recognized that Bowyers was a completely different kind of company, whose values were quite different from those of Walls. This is not to say that Bowyers recruited me into a head-on battle, specifically trying to take on Walls; it is simply the case that every commercial design project takes account of all competitors. It is only for the purpose of this book that I am drawing a direct comparison between Bowyers and Walls.

We focused on the wholesome, nutritious abundance of Bowyers' products, and specifically distanced the company from any perceptions of 'factories' and 'processed' foods. Bowyers are based in Wiltshire, and we brought the feeling of this rural county to the cities with their products. The obvious tonal family to communicate these values was Group III – the autumnal qualities of substance, abundance and a rich harvest were exactly what was required. Thus all the perceptions of environmental awareness and humanely run abattoirs were inherent.

Since the packaging of sausages is always effected in a design which allows the products to be seen, I then applied the basic principle of contrasting complementary colours across the range to emphasize their colour, specifying that a warm autumnal green should predominate on the sausage pack, especially around the edges of the design, where it directly abutted the sight of the sausages themselves. The green would emphasize the red meatiness of the product – green being complementary to red.

On the same principle, I specified an autumnal dark blue (quite different from Walls' Winter navy) for pies, so that the blue could bring out the rich golden tones of the pastry. We warmed up and enriched the yellow of Bowyers' 'sunrise' logo and banned all black lettering from the pack. A warm red was also present, in small touches and in some of the lettering, so the whole range presented a very balanced picture.

CHOOSING COLOURS THAT WORK TOGETHER

I shudder to think of the amount of money which is spent in the lengthy and essentially empirical process of choosing colours. The most common colour mistakes derive from the belief that success comes from a particular colour, rather than understanding that colour itself is a constantly dynamic element, whose properties change in relation to a variety of factors – most notably the relationships among the shades, tints and tones themselves. A designer might hit upon a perfect colour to express a proposition. Everyone feels comfortable with the choice; then, as the designing proceeds, it does not seem to fulfil its initial promise. As time goes on and deadlines approach, someone starts questioning the initial choice, and it will be adjusted in some way – then the other colours on the pack need some adjustment. Time is running short, compromises have to be made. By the time the pack gets to the market research stage, it is rather like the Philosopher's Axe – is it still the same design?

If the market research results are not good – what then? The designer, we must assume, gave it her best shot first time. What can she do now? If the project is not scrapped, there is only one answer, and that is to keep trying alternatives. Eventually, by good luck, she will come up with a colour scheme which meets with the approval of the market research respondents, and the pack will go into the marketplace. But no one knows what, precisely, it was about the pack that appealed. So the perception that colour is an unpredictable matter of subjective opinion is reinforced. Everyone concerned will post-rationalize and attribute the success to some particular factor, place their interpretation on the results. They may or may not be right – but what is certain is that the whole exercise has cost the client a great deal of money, and the designers much heartache.

Instead of focusing on each colour, and attempting to find one which appeals in itself every time, it is vital to recognize that, once you have decided on the core colour, then every other colour choice must be viewed, not in terms of its own appeal, but in its relationship to the core colour. The colours will then mutually enhance.

The biggest challenge I have to face in this context is in convincing designers that pure white and black are not neutral and should not just be used as a matter of course. Perhaps it is because the traditional starting point of any graphic design project was invariably a black pencil and a white paper sketch pad. Black and white are so ingrained in designers' minds that they simply will not believe me when I tell them that a white background, or black lettering, can destroy the whole project. (The Simple packaging, described earlier, does not have black lettering.)

Black is always thought to be the most legible, but again this is an illusion. Black lettering is the most legible only on a white background. It will work well on any other Group IV (Winter) background, but it behaves entirely differently in a warm-toned colour scheme. On, let us say, a yellow or orange background, deep violet or dark blue lettering will be more legible because of the phenomenon, explained in Part One, of complementary colours. The one pair of complementary colours I would not recommend in a context where ease of reading is an issue is red and green – one in seven of the male population is colour-blind and inability to distinguish red and green is a common form.

NEATLY PACKAGED | 163

PRACTICALITIES OF PRINTING

There is also a very practical basis for this attachment to black: it is the easiest and cheapest from the printer's point of view. Printing machines are usually inked up with black as a matter of course, so any other colour costs the client more, if only from the purely practical point of view of the time it takes to clean down the machines.

But printing is an extremely complex business in itself, and colour printing is fraught with its own problems. The four primary colours in printing are cyan (a light, bright blue), magenta, yellow and black. These are known, rather confusingly, as CYMK – using K as the initial for black because B could also stand for blue. There are various printing colour systems which will provide a formula for mixing the precise colour required, but 99 per cent of the time the printer will match the required colour by eye, rather than by formula.

Some small printers will not do colour printing at all; some will, but not beyond the four colour process, which is very limited. The larger companies have an extraordinary battery of modern technology, and can produce any colour you wish – but the familiar pursed lips and indrawn breath of the builder making an estimate in your home is as nothing to that of the printer asked to produce accurate colours outside of a very small range. I am afraid I am not greatly loved by the printing fraternity in general – they know I am going to be trouble – but those who really love their work and welcome a challenge are a real joy to work with, and they, and I, always enjoy a delicious sense of satisfaction when we achieve something harmonious, unusual and effective.

One of the hazards of colour matching by eye is a phenomenon known as metamerism. This is when two colours which match perfectly under certain lighting conditions no longer match in a different light. We have all seen the way the colours of the merchandise inside a shop are completely different when we look at them outside the door, in daylight. Design studios always have different types of light, to enable them to check the colours. How the printer arrives at the desired colour will have a major bearing on the situation. One solution to the problem of metamerism is to specify the colour in terms of the light reflectance co-ordinates. This, however, requires a spectrophotometer – a computer for analysing colour – which is a piece of equipment only the large printing firms have. Most of the time, in practice, it is down to the printer's expertise.

Supposing, for example, a designer has specified Pantone 302C. This is a warm dark blue made up of two of the Pantone Corporation's own products – Process Blue and Reflex Blue – with some black, and it would therefore be deemed 'a special' and charged accordingly. The printer could achieve a roughly similar result, though inevitably lacking in intensity, by a different route: using three of the four primaries in the proportions of 100 cyan to 30 magenta to 70 black. Alternatively, he could use the four colours: 100 cyan to 20 yellow to 50 magenta to 40 black.

The printer's decisions have a major bearing on both long-term performance of the colour and on budget. I remember once being told by a printer, whose second attempt to produce the colours I required for a complex brochure was still woefully wide of the mark, that a perfect reproduction could not be done with fewer than nine basic colours. His competitor did a perfect job using five.

One of the unexpected bonuses I discovered in harmonizing colours in the tonal groups described in this book is that, although colours will still change under different lighting conditions, they retain their harmony. It is as if they all move together. I am currently working with a colour physicist who is using very sophisticated computers, to understand better why this should be. It is a fascinating project.

We are also addressing, and my colleague has solved, another major problem in colour design: that of colour changes occurring across different media. These days, most design houses are equipped with computers, and computer-aided design ('CAD') is virtually the norm. The problem is that colour in a computer is light, whilst colour in printing is ink, colour in textiles is dye and colour in interior design is paint. They are all mixed differently; computer monitors vary in their presentation of colours, too. It is very difficult to be sure of the colour you want on the computer screen to start with, and then, when you try to print it out, it changes. Specifying it for the other media changes it even further. One can sympathize with designers or printers playing safe, working with the good old-fashioned eye and sticking to a relatively small number of familiar colours. But solutions to these problems are on the horizon

CHAPTER EIGHTEEN

Man-made Environments

The first packaging project I ever worked on amazed me: the pack was about 4in x 2in x 1in (10cm x 5cm x 2.5cm) and was required to carry a wealth of values and messages, which had to be communicated instantly, to potential purchasers. I had just completed a major interior design project for a large retail chain, covering hundreds of stores throughout Britain, before tackling this cold-cure pack. At the end of a particularly trying day, I threw up my hands in frustration:

'I cannot believe that anything this size can be so complicated! Give me 350 shops to colour any time!'

For a while, I let that idea grow, and really imagined that three-dimensional design was easier; perhaps I even thought it was less important than the complexities of graphics. The idea of all the millions which might be lost if we got the packaging wrong turned my head.

This misconception did not last long; I rapidly realized that interior design – creating environments within which every human activity occurs – is the most important aspect of colour psychology in commerce. The issues go beyond the purely commercial. Most people live and work indoors, and if the colours of their surroundings are disharmonious, too bland or too hectic, everyone will be either, as I have said before, drained or strained. The colours in offices, shops, hotels, restaurants, factories, hospitals, schools and other institutions – all types of public building – can create the best environment to support and encourage human endeavour, or provide the major contributory factor to increasing stress levels (a serious cause of illness and absenteeism) and reducing productivity.

I found it depressing one day, when I attended an international exhibition for professional interior designers, at Earls Court in London. All the companies seemed to be offering the same thing. Eventually I asked the representative of one of our major flooring manufacturers about how colour decisions were made and colour palettes devised; was serious consideration ever given to questions of colour? He replied, with a slight shrug,

'Oh, I don't know – we just have a look at what the competition is doing and more or less follow suit.'

GROUP I FRIENDLINESS
AND WARMTH WAS
APPROPRIATE FOR THE
BT SHOPS.

BRITISH TELECOM

I complained at the beginning of Part Four about cavalier attitudes to colour amongst professionals. It is often only when they have arbitrarily discarded a colour that they discover how effective it was. The general public registers colour strongly, although they do not necessarily analyse the reasons behind an apparently inexplicable gut reaction.

A striking example of this was British Telecom's experience in the 1980s. Although a telephone box is not exactly a building, it is public, and there was a great outcry in Britain when the familiar red ones were replaced. Originally, when the telephone service was the province of the General Post Office, both telephone boxes and letter-boxes were painted bright red, presumably in the interests of visibility. Red is a friendly colour and everyone loved the warmth and familiarity. On a purely practical level, a telephone box can be a draughty place on a cold winter's night, and the perception of warmth in the colour was helpful. What British Telecom failed to understand is that red is also a stimulating colour, encouraging extroversion and conversation. Conviviality is good for a company which derives revenue from the length of time people talk to each other. Even the improved service in public telephones, the rapid repair of vandalized boxes and the increased numbers of them available did not really mollify a public who wanted their red telephone boxes back. The company halted the removal programme and restored those few which were left.

Later, when BT decided to revamp its corporate identity, it compounded the problem. At that point the predominant influence in the company's public personality was autumnal; it had a fleet of vans painted rich, warm yellow, with warm, dark blue lettering – very visible and very British. The brief to the designers was to modernize the company's image and repackage it as a major international organization, working at the cutting edge of modern technology across the globe. This could have been achieved with a Group IV palette which, if it had replaced the old colours properly, would have more than compensated for the removal of the red phone boxes, and the subsequent loss of the yellow vans; the general public would have recognized BT as an authoritative organization, efficient and reliable, moving with the times. The idea of using the powerful symbolism of the red, white and blue to communicate the concept of latter-day empire-building was entirely appropriate.

There might also have been a case for using Group I (Spring) colours. Their clarity would have been a positive factor, and they would have communicated the idea that the new BT was friendly and caring, but still modern and efficient.

Unfortunately, what emerged was a jumble of Spring and Winter tones which conspired to communicate a lack of conviction and did nothing to endear the company to its customers. (It was not helped by a leak to the tabloid press, months before the company was ready to announce its plans, essentially putting BT on the defensive.) The livery on the glass and metal kiosks became the corporate cold red (going towards magenta) for the pay phones and a vivid lime green for the Phonecard boxes. This application of colour, in small quantities, on the metal kiosks was an entirely different matter from having warm red telephone boxes. Most of the time, the red and the green stand side by side and present a very harsh combination; furthermore, rather like the pink shopping centre mentioned earlier, neither colour has worn well. There was more: the yellow of the fleet of vans was replaced with grey; a light, Group I grey. When it became apparent that these vans were virtually invisible at twilight, however, BT's designers did devise a brilliant solution to the problem: the company logo of a slightly overweight Pan was painted on the sides in luminous white paint.

There was so much opprobrium heaped upon the heads of BT and their designers that they convened a gathering, which I attended, at the

Chartered Society of Designers to discuss the project. They were not given an easy ride. One young man on the podium was asked to explain the decision to paint the vans grey and said, rather unconvincingly,

'We researched the visibility of colours, and that shade of grey is much more visible than yellow.'

He brought the house down.

I felt I did not want to raise any questions at that event. I admired everyone concerned in the project for facing up to the criticism. They were obviously extremely uncomfortable, but they did manage to justify many of the design decisions; they were not just talking about colour. It seemed to me they recognized that they had not made a good job of choosing the colours; they did not need anyone to tell them that. The implementation of that new identity – new telephone boxes, vans, stationery, etc., etc. – cost approximately £60 million, so the colours had to stay. In time they acquired a certain familiarity which mitigates in favour of the company's image, for as long as it is allied to improved service. There is no equity in the corporate colours themselves; they have been made to work, rather than being inherently powerful.

Later, I was asked to provide a palette for the designers working on the BT shops. I explained to them that, since the two core colours of BT – the red and the blue – were at odds with each other, there was an inherent contradiction. We would have to decide whether to go with the Group I blue (which predominated) or the Group IV red. Everyone agreed that Group I friendliness and warmth were more desirable in the shops at that point than the cold efficiency of Group IV, which could be negated by the Group I corporate blue, and come across as hard and uncaring. I devised a palette of Group I tones, but I was not involved in the implementation; I understand it was well received, although it has since changed again.

HER MAJESTY'S PRISON SERVICE

One of my most interesting projects was devising colours for the Vulnerable Prisoners' Units for HM Prison Service. There are those who feel that time and money should not be spent on making prisons a pleasant place to be, but if the alternative is simply to focus on containment, and take no advantage of the opportunity to influence and improve attitudes of inmates while they are captive, it seems to me unlikely that the overall situation will ever improve. Prison is not, I assure you, pleasant.

The law says that any prisoner's request for segregation on the grounds of feeling at risk from other prisoners must be granted. This is commonly known as 'Rule 43', after the relevant section of the Act, and Rule 43 prisoners are generally paedophiles, sex offenders, informers, possibly ex-policemen – anyone who feels under threat. The Vulnerable Prisoners' Unit, in architectural terms, could be anything from part of a wing in a Victorian prison to a wholly designated modern building.

I had often noticed, whenever I saw the inside of a prison on TV, that there appeared to be a predominance of yellow on the walls. This is probably an expression of colour symbolism: 'Let's brighten the place up a bit – yellow is the colour of sunshine.' In principle there is nothing wrong with that idea. When I actually visited a prison for the first time, I found that there was indeed a predominance of yellow, but that it was a very strong lemon yellow – an acid, Group IV tone – and it was juxtaposed with warm colours, which negated its uplifting possibilities. I particularly remember one staircase, newly painted in this yellow, with bright warm tan skirting board and banister; it looked fresh and clean, but the two colours clashed to a psychologically highly stressful degree.

Since the palette I was to provide had to work positively in architecture of all styles and periods, in buildings of all shapes and sizes, this was a project where the concept of psychological mode really came into its own. Indeed it was the only possible approach. The starting point was the innate vulnerability of the inmates. Most of them are fearful, many depressed; feelings of hopelessness can overtake them, and suicide is a very real danger. There are also those who are filled with resentment and anger. Some have not been found guilty of any crime, as they are on remand, awaiting trial.

It was felt that there should, if possible, be a change in the atmosphere between the inside of the cells and the public areas, so that a prisoner might feel some sense of the cell being a sanctuary, after the possible stress of, say, group therapy or other communal activity. I was able to accede to that request by devising a palette from a different season for the cells (with very clear warnings about not using these colours anywhere else).

The other element which it was important to accommodate was the attitude of the prison officers; they needed to be supported in their endeavours too. Essentially they are engaged in keeping the peace, and theirs is a very stressful job.

After I had analysed all these moods and feelings, put them into a pot and stirred them up, I came to the conclusion that the best tonal family, or season, of colours to reflect and support them overall was Group I – Spring. This created a framework of lightness, even optimism; it would lift the atmosphere and remove any perception of heaviness. For the cells, I went to Group III – Autumn. These colours were also warm, but more solid, and supportive to the individual in moments of introspection. The majority of the British population (and therefore, I had to assume, the prison population) is linked to Autumn, so most of them would feel reasonably at home with such tones. Also, since both seasons are warm, this gave me scope for preventing a great clash between the autumnal tone on the inside of the cell doors and the colour of the outside of them – which related to the Group I-oriented corridors.

Once that decision was made, it was a matter of analysing the required mode in each different area. Sometimes areas double up, but in the main they are used for broadly similar activities. I recommended sets of colours for each area, as follows:

1. Mentally stimulating, for use in classrooms, workshops and administrative areas.

2. Physically stimulating, for use in the canteen, leisure areas, gymnasium and workshops.

3. Mentally soothing, for the library, chapel, hospital, reception area and staff rest rooms.

4. A balance of optimism and containment (warm yellow and dark blue) for therapy rooms.

5. A supporting palette for corridors, stairways, showers, ablutions and dual-purpose areas.

6. A palette based on slightly less institutional principles for the cells. The colour on the walls was a soft pink, with a hint of apricot – not at all a baby pink, nor excessively feminine.

Many of the colours specified overlapped, but for each palette they were designated A, the core colour to denote the predominant mood, B for secondary application (window frames, doors, etc.) and C, to be used in small doses as accent colours. By altering the proportions we altered the colour balance, which enabled us to achieve maximum flexibility without using too many colours and complicating the whole project to the point where it would not be applied.

The fact that every single shade, tone or tint throughout related to the same tonal group meant that there was an underlying harmony which underpinned the project and created the atmosphere, holding true even if someone made a mistake and applied a colour in the wrong place. It was actually quite simple, once it was presented in a clear operational manual. The Home Office saw it as a very cost-effective way of improving the situation, because the prisons have to be painted anyway and the colour of the paint does not materially affect the cost, unless it is not a standard colour, which I avoided.

Some years ago, West Yorkshire Police, working with academics from the University of Leeds, tried an experiment, wherein they painted a strip cell (a cell stripped of all furniture and anything which could be used to harm the prisoner, into which severely disturbed prisoners are placed) pink, in an effort to soothe the disturbed prisoner. This was presumably a follow-up to similar experiments in San José, California, where various colours were used to assess the effects on behaviour. The English experiment more or less came to naught and the cause of colour psychology was put back another few years.

I watched the TV news report and was greatly disheartened at the crude definition of pink. The whole cell had been painted in a bubble-gum pink, even more intense than the one on the aforementioned shopping centre. It also appeared to be a gloss paint. This intense colour is essentially stimulating, whether in a positive or a negative way, and could not possibly soothe anyone – not even a Winter-linked personality, who would have a positive relationship with shocking pink. The colour theoretically reflects a concept which is slightly incongruous in itself, that of feminine aggression or, more positively, assertion. I find this problematical, but the fact remains that shocking pink, or fuchsia, has enjoyed great popularity throughout the twentieth century – coincidentally the period that has seen women on the march, and particularly in the 1980s, when the women's movement reached its zenith.

I suggest that, if the West Yorkshire police had tried the same experiment with a much softer, carefully evaluated tone of pink, they would have achieved very positive results. Whilst they were at it, they could have investigated what certain shades of blue would do for the disturbed prisoner, and green too. The pink would soothe physically – 'I still don't agree, but I haven't got the energy to fight'; the blue would soothe mentally – 'All right, tell me again; I feel more reasonable now'; and the green would bring about a balance of the two.

COLOURS IN TRANSIT

Another area where tension is endemic is in major travel centres, such as airport terminals, railway stations, even underground stations. The inside of the aircraft, train or ship is equally tense. When a person travels, he or she is implicitly abdicating control over circumstances to someone else. That is a relevant point in all forms of travel, but we do not spend as much time in, for example, a tube or an overland railway station as we do, generally speaking, in an airport. The next time you travel, look around you at the behaviour of your fellow travellers. People are reluctant to go too far away from the information screens and constantly refer to them, in case anything might have changed in the thirty seconds or so since they last looked. You can see the tension in the set of the mouth and the body language; babies and small children are more inclined to cry; everyone is under pressure.

Why, then, do you suppose, do designers use such stimulating colours in this context? It could be appropriate to focus on the pleasurable anticipation of travelling, but it is risky; if you are going to take that approach, it is essential that you really know what you are doing with colour. There is enough excitement already, inside the minds of travellers before they even leave home, in the inevitably busy atmosphere and essential clock watching, in the underlying fears of something going wrong and, these days, in the battery of shops and other franchised businesses screaming at you to come and buy while you are waiting. The last time I went through Gatwick Airport, I sat down quietly to wait, and found myself surrounded by strong green and purple geometric patterns in the carpet, clashing with rosy red seating. I was not at all comfortable.

I have done some work in this context – the English terminal of the Channel Tunnel and for London Underground – but not nearly as much as I would like. Changing attitudes in very large, monolithic organizations is a slow process, and I have had to learn to be grateful for any opportunity to insert the thin end of the wedge.

LADBROKE'S

One project where I was given free rein was very recently, when the laws on gambling – another psychological mode which is loaded with complexities – were changed to give everyone a level playing field in the light of the National Lottery. It was the first major change in Britain in thirty-one years, since betting shops were legalized in 1963. All the major bookmakers began to re-examine their whole business, and how they would present themselves when they became deregulated. Before, they had to have closed shop-fronts and submit to a rather arcane and very long list of restrictions. The implications of deregulation in gambling, and of modern attitudes to the field of leisure in general, are still being addressed, as the major players consider which directions their businesses will go in future.

One of the largest chains of betting shops is owned by Ladbroke's. Their first move was to commission designers to refurbish all their premises, initially to streamline the process and reduce the amount of time a shop was out of commission while it was being done. They recognized that it was time to think in terms of economy of scale and cost effectiveness, with uniformity across the whole chain. It was not a simple matter, as the shops were all so different architecturally, but the designers did a good job and, by the time they had completed the fourth prototype, everyone felt that they had got it more or less right.

Except for one thing. The Chairman was not happy with the colours. He had heard of me, but could not quite remember where; he instructed his assistant to search the files and they eventually tracked me down.

I was briefed to provide an analysis of the colours and where necessary to suggest alternatives, the only real provisos being to be wary of blue, as both their major competitors had recently updated their image, leaning heavily on dark blue, and to remember that the company had recently completed a corporate identity update. I must not change the new Ladbroke's red. This was Pantone 185C, a bright, warm scarlet. It is a pure Group I Spring tone, a lovely colour and very popular with printers and graphic designers, but I had reservations about it for Ladbroke's. I said nothing and reserved judgement until I had examined the whole picture.

I mentioned in Chapter Seventeen the difficulty of translating colour from one medium to another. Nowhere is this problem more marked than in interior design. ICI Paints have made a big effort in this direction, in establishing the Colour Dimensions Association. Having bought from the Scandinavian Institute, in Sweden, the right to use their Natural Colour

System, under the trade name Dulux Colour Dimensions, they provide the formula for every colour in their range and work together with manufacturers of textiles, plastics, tiles, flooring, carpets, etc., to bring more accurate colour matching into the world of interior design. It is a step in the right direction, but it has a long way to go yet.

The Ladbroke's shop I first visited had about five different versions of red, but the precisely specified tone of the corporate red itself was nowhere to be seen. They were supposed to match it exactly, but the seating bore no relation to the fascia; the signage had several different reds, and the waste-bins offered another alternative.

The first point to be made in this audit of the colours, therefore, was to advise Ladbroke's of the potential for stress in the colour red, and how strong was the negative influence of having several disparate reds in a relatively small space.

The second – even more negative – element was the predominance of grey. The shop was extremely elegant and very 'designer' (as the 1980s phrase went). It presented a mixture between Group I, which theoretically related to the new corporate red, and Group IV. The carpet was two tones of cold grey, the paintwork was grey, and the housing for all the TV screens appeared at first glance to be black, but was in fact a dark, inky, Winter grey-blue. Much of the signage was white lettering out of a black background, designed to recall the signage on racecourses by using the same typeface.

It was clever, and people admired it. However, it was rather cold, and all wrong for the concept of gambling. Much of the admiration derived from a phenomenon known as the Hawthorne Effect, whereby any change is initially seen as an improvement, even if it has no innately superior value. The worst colour to use in a betting shop is grey, as I am sure readers can readily understand from what has already been explained in this book. Grey encourages us to draw in and hoard resources, in case we are in for a long winter. This is not at all the frame of mind which will encourage us to splash out and 'have a flutter'. The best colour in this context is probably green, but there is so much superstition surrounding green, and gambling is almost entirely a matter of luck and superstition, that the company would not be keen to use it.

The report I presented to Ladbroke's explained all of the above, and included two palettes: one developed the colour scheme into Group I, to bring everything into line with the corporate red, the other adjusted all the tones into Group IV, in line with the predominant influence already there. The implications of the two alternatives were explained in depth.

Unknown to me, the Chairman's initial doubts about the colours had been entirely focused on the grey. He just kept saying,

'There is too much grey.'

No one was allowed to tell me that, so when my report homed in on exactly that point, and explained the rationale behind the instinct, the company was impressed.

THIS NEW LADBROKE'S BETTING SHOP IS AN IMPROVEMENT ON THE OLD, BUT BLACK AND GREY DO NOTHING TO SUPPORT THE NOTION OF 'HAVING A FLUTTER'.

WITH THE COLOURS WARMED UP, THE WHOLE ATMOSPHERE LIFTS.

I also advised that the Ladbroke's red had previously been an autumnal tone, and indeed the predominant influence in the shops refurbished immediately prior to the new design was autumnal. I explained that this communicated values of strength, tradition and reliability, allied with warmth, which perhaps it might be advisable to reconsider.

Ladbroke's recognized that the Winter palette was not appropriate and readily discarded that. At the same time, they could see that there was something missing in the Spring palette. Now that the whole palette had been developed from the core red, the harmony was very clear to see, but it did not quite add up to the picture Ladbroke's had of itself. They retained me to work with the designers and we presented them with an autumnal palette, built around their traditional red, as an alternative to the Spring palette. As soon as they saw it, they recognized themselves:

'That's us! That says Ladbroke's.'

The fifth prototype had all the same design features, except for the colours, and it was a completely different shop. We sorted out all the reds, and the predominant colour inside became an autumnal greenish-blue, replacing the grey. I specified a tone which combined the reliability of blue with the reassurance of green, without falling into the twin traps of either – the competitors' colour and the perception of bad luck. We rationalized and simplified the whole colour scheme, and it worked well. The designers were sceptical at first, particularly when I stuck to my guns about the removal of all black and grey, but otherwise they were very co-operative, and gracious in their comments at the end of the project.

The bonus for Ladbroke's derived from the potential for increasing their business, not just reducing their costs – which had been their initial objective. It is to be hoped that the new colour scheme will provide a positive aspect of the company's image for years to come. If colours are right, they stand the test of time.

CHAPTER NINETEEN

The Colour of Money

The psychology of retailing is very skilled and, as we know, includes, in addition to the design of the shops and packaging of the merchandise, clever layout techniques to ensure that the natural flow of people takes them to every section and leads them gently, but with deadly accuracy, towards the merchandise in such a way as to maximize sales. Manufacturers fight for the right to have their product displayed at the most effective level (between waist and eye level is the place you are most likely to register a brand). The old days, when we went into a shop, walked up to the counter, behind which were the shopkeeper and most of the merchandise, and asked for what we wanted, are all but gone. These days we help ourselves; everything is laid before us in the most enticing way possible and impulse purchases are a major part of the exercise (as is the cost of security, when shoplifting seems so easy and so tempting), so as shoppers we have to employ clever tactics ourselves to resist the retailer's ploys.

We know that it is never a good idea to go food shopping on an empty stomach. We know that we must make out our shopping list before we leave home, so that we will only buy what we need – and we try to concentrate on just the items on the list. But how often do we stick to our good intentions? It is all so clever, and so irresistible. For instance, just as we have become thoroughly familiar with the layout in our local supermarket, so that we can almost go around it and find everything we need on automatic pilot, we will go in there one day and find that the staff have worked all night to rearrange the whole thing. This means we have to go looking for everything afresh – try doing that without making any impulse purchases!

Supermarkets are not totally without scruples, however. When large numbers of customers complained that displaying sweets and chocolates at the check-out, the one place where people had to stand and wait, was creating major problems for young mothers, trying to withstand the demands of bored and fractious children, many of them discontinued the policy.

ASPIRATIONS IN SHOPPING

Retailers recognize that when we go shopping we are not simply buying an item which we need, we are tuning into our deepest aspirations and buying into a whole lifestyle every time. Buying anything is a new beginning, an expression of hope. The experience is loaded with psychological complexities. This has long been acknowledged: in the old days, people bought their clothes, for example, from more individual shops, and ladies' fashions were always sold in the most elegant of surroundings by women who called you 'Madam' and gave you their undivided attention. Men bought their clothes from tailors who made it their business to get to know their customers very well. In both cases, people were made to feel very good about themselves when they went shopping, although one would often hesitate to enter the hallowed portals of some shops.

These days, the whole emphasis has shifted. No one needs to feel diffident about going into any shop any more – they have opened up to all comers and their aim is to draw you in, like a magnet. Once you are in, they will more or less ignore you and let you get on with the business of choosing by yourself. The concept of service has altered so much in the last thirty years or so that many older people feel it no longer exists; even banks and building societies tend to describe the services they are offering as 'products'. Retail surroundings are much more subtly designed and present a microcosm of a whole world, or a whole philosophy, to which each person responds on a personal level. Even though much of it is fake, rather more like a theme park than a genuine presentation, it works. These days we are more likely to recognize quickly which is our kind of shop and which is not.

In the 1980s, the desired atmosphere was glitzy and sophisticated – all about glamour and material aspiration. Shops were very spacious, with a preponderance of mirrors and chrome, cool ceramic tiles on the floor, plenty of black and dramatic touches of colour. Grey – the perfect Winter neutral, supporting those perceptions of modernity and originality – was the 'in' colour and retailers used it lavishly to show how cool they were. One of the reasons it became such a popular colour in the commercial marketplace is that it tempered all the naked materialism of the era, and unconsciously reflected the developing fear and underlying doubts: can this boom last? Is it right? Grey was, as we know, not in itself a good colour in the retailing environment. Its value lay in supporting Group IV – Winter.

In the 1990s the mood has changed and all the major multiple stores are going for Autumn colours, exposed beams, varnished wooden floors, copper, timber veneers and a more earthy, even ethnic feel. The overall mood is autumnal, and the styles of Mexico and South America have come into their own. We are more aware of the Third World, and the excesses of the 1980s are no longer considered acceptable. Naked consumerism is out, purity of substance is in. The Japanese company Muji, with its entire merchandise in black and white, and no frills whatever (although not autumnal; the Body Shop, Gap, Timberland, River Island – all are examples of the mood. Even the ultra-chic Giorgio Armani's elegant Emporio follows this design philosophy.

In the twentieth century, society's mood has tended to change every decade, and the history of design divides up very neatly into the 1920s, '50s, '80s, etc. It is impossible to predict with absolute accuracy (much of

MOTHERCARE'S IMAGE
HAD LOST ITS AUTHORITY
OVER THE YEARS AS THE
PURITY OF THE ORIGINAL
SPRING COLOURS HAD
BEEN DILUTED.

the science of fashion forecasting inevitably becomes a matter of creating self-fulfilling prophecies), but I would not be surprised if the current mood held for a little longer this time. When the sea change does occur, I would expect to see a mood of cheery regeneration and optimism return. This is likely to be expressed in Spring colours and design features, echoing a mood reminiscent of the 1950s.

Some companies, of course, do not present themselves in autumnal robes. It would not be appropriate for them. An example of accurate use of colour is the Virgin Group. For their airline, initially presenting a new and friendlier approach to air travel, they chose warm red and grey. In some applications the red drifts into Autumn, but for the most part the Virgin Airways' offer is Spring – absolutely right. Young, friendly, lively, they cheekily set about puncturing myths and mystique propagated by many of the older airlines, whose focus on efficiency, reliability and trust-worthiness was presumably designed to reassure nervous passengers, but also in the process offered a justification for high prices. For their Virgin Megastores, however, where the focus is on the very latest in modern technology and trend-setting music, and all that is associated with it, the company chose Group IV – Winter – glitz, with a heavy use of chrome and plenty of black. Again, exactly right.

Three examples of companies which went against the fashionable flow and chose to focus accurately on their own charcteristics and values come to mind: I recommended Spring colours for all three.

MOTHERCARE

The first one, in the 1980s, was Mothercare. Founded in the 1960s, it pio-neered the concept 'Everything for the mother- to-be and her child'.

Before that, pregnant women were generally expected not to make a fuss and, since pregnancy was a temporary condition, it was considered foolish to spend money on clothes that would make women look and feel good during this vital period: they should just loosen their existing skirts (using safety pins instead of the buttons and zips to hold them up), or wear completely shapeless garments which tended to create the impression of a faceless blur, and get through it as best they could.

I sometimes wonder if Mothercare did not contribute more than we realize to modern feminism, when it presented clothes especially designed for the purpose, with expanding waistlines and elegant detail to draw the eye away from the 'bulge', at prices that people could afford, justifying the purchase. This enabled women to say, 'Look at me! I look good. I'm pregnant!' The idea rapidly developed that women could still function normally, be attractive, feel comfortable and dress well when they were pregnant. Everyone began to acknowledge the unique beauty of a pregnant woman.

Allied to that was Mothercare's understanding of the terror that grips the novice mother as she realizes that she is bringing a new and very demanding little person into the world, who will be dependent on her and about whom she knows absolutely nothing. Grandma is full of advice, of course, and so is the midwife for a while, but after that, where did the young first-time mother go for guidance? (In those days, fathers were rather sidelined in all this; their role was to make enough money to support the family.) Mothercare opened its doors, with absolutely everything taken care of. Young parents flocked to their stores to buy cute baby clothes, cots, prams, pushchairs, feeding equipment, nappies and, crucially, advice – there was nothing the company had not thought of. The young mother never needed to go to any other kind of shop until her child was five years old.

Twenty-five years on, the company had rather lost its way. It had developed into the toy and clothes market for children up to twelve years old, and diversified in various directions; competitors had sprung up and established themselves. Suddenly Mothercare was no longer the authority, the friendly expert to which every young parent automatically turned. Its core offer had been diluted to the point of being obscured.

The five colours which Mothercare had always used, in a variety of applications – on shopping bags and signage, and incorporated into the decor – wére called the 'sweet pea colours'. Pink, blue, yellow, green and lilac, they captured the essence of what Mothercare stood for.

Before I was commissioned, Mothercare had brought in designers to address the problem of an apparent loss of authority. The designers came up with the ultimate authority colour – dark blue. The tone they chose was a strong colour, similar to the one previously described as 'pharmaceutical blue'. Applying it in the shops, they instinctively then recognized that the walls would have to be painted white to harmonize with it. The result was, in the words of one less than delighted executive, 'Now we look more like Medicare than Mothercare!' At the same time, all the other colours, still in Spring tones, had suddenly been converted from young and friendly to frivolous and immature.

When I arrived at Mothercare's head office I was interested to note the pure Autumn quality of everything – and virtually everyone – I saw. The reception area was exposed brick, with stone features, tan leather chairs and touches of Autumn colour. Throughout the building, most of the tones were autumnal and the senior management team themselves, most of them with brown or hazel eyes, demonstrated archetypal Autumn attitudes throughout the meeting. Since the company had by now conducted a radical reassessment of its whole operation, it would not have been out of the question to move all the colours in the stores into autumnal Group III, which would have reflected the values of the company. I explained all this to the board, but recommended that they stick to Group I, Spring. Everyone, whatever their own season or their age, entering a Mothercare shop, goes into the psychological mode of youth. A Spring environment would be more likely to create the appropriate mood in the stores.

The first thing I addressed was the 'sweet pea colours'. They had drifted all over the place over the years; originally all Group I, only the blue and the lilac remained true, the pink having become a Group IV candy pink and the green resembling pistachio ice cream, also in Group IV; the yellow, now a very warm, almost buttery tone, had gone over firmly to Group III. I adjusted the yellow, the pink and the green back into Spring.

Then the question of emphasizing the time-honoured authority of Mothercare had to be addressed. I endorsed the original designers' instinct which led to the dark blue, but explained that it had to be a Group I tone. Since there are no really dark colours in Group I, nor is any of them very strong, I specified a blue which was darker and stronger than the 'sweet pea' version, and recommended that it be used in more quantity, so that the balance could be perceptibly shifted towards it. In the context of the whole Spring ethos, this colour communicated authority and reliability in a friendly environment.

It worked very well and everyone was delighted. Sadly, however, it was not long after that that the recession hit hard, and fundamental attitudes in commerce were re-evaluated. Mothercare changed its entire management, and the new team decided to redesign it all over again. I was not involved.

COMET

Another company which was on the crest of a wave in the 1980s was Comet Electrical Goods. At that time, every electrical goods store presented itself in warm red and cold grey. It was difficult to tell them apart, and going into the shops was not a pleasant experience. The merchandise always seemed to be extremely cluttered, often with banks of television sets, all switched on, and endless hard chunks of black or grey technological wizardry, creating a strain the moment you walked in. This was about the time that the American concept of megastores, congregated all together on out-of-town sites, was really taking hold in Britain. Comet had commissioned designers to come up with an original approach to the design of these superstores, and had one completed, which was greatly admired.

One of the directors heard about my work and, since everyone recognized that, elegant as it was, there was still room for improvement in the first store, he invited me to talk to the board. The first question they asked me was,

'What is the colour of money?'

'Green,' I replied. 'Is that it? Is the meeting over?'

We all laughed and the meeting was far from over. They commissioned me to come up with a colour scheme for the new megastore. But they could only give me a few days, as the designers were presenting a colour scheme then, and the company wished to have the opportunity to consider both alternatives. I had no idea who the designers were. Of course, I knew that there would be time later to develop the colour scheme at more leisure, but nevertheless, I had to get it more or less right first time.

The building itself was a vast, cavernous, warehouse type of place, with no natural daylight. The nature of the merchandise inevitably created a buzz, and implicit in the offer was cheap and cheerful (remember, as opposed to 'cheap and tacky') value for money. The majority of potential customers – i.e. the target market – were young people.

It did not take long to make the decision to go into Group I. Indeed, there was no viable alternative; I had probably already made that basic decision before I left the meeting. Since Group I colours have a lot of light in them, this went some way towards countering the absence of natural light in the store; the Spring environment also served to convert the inherent activity and movement in the closely stacked merchandise from a potential strain to a buzz of optimistic excitement.

The layout of the store was as follows: the whole of the left-hand side was designated the 'white goods' area. This is the trade name for domestic appliances such as fridges, freezers, cookers, washing machines, etc., which tend to be predominantly white. The other side of the store presented the 'brown goods' – the more leisure-oriented items such as TV and videos, music systems, camcorders and other gadgetry. The decision had already been made to use very large signs in each section to guide the customer towards specific goods. The cashiers were to be located right in the middle of the wide central aisle.

Having established that it was to be a Spring colour scheme, I specified a cream paint for the walls and the ceiling – the background colour, warm, very light and fairly neutral. I then decided that, as 'white goods' are all about work and 'brown goods' all about leisure, we had to create a perception of efficiency and labour saving on the left-hand side of the store and a sense of enjoyment and fun on the right. The obvious bias, then, was for blue on the left and red on the right. Pure red would have created far too much stimulation, so I specified a light orange for the signage on that side. The pure Spring blue on the left was perfect.

Then I had to find a way to draw them together and balance the overall scheme, introducing some longer wavelengths on the blue side and some shorter ones on the orange.

The opportunity to do this presented itself in the flooring. The 'white goods' floor was to be vinyl and the 'brown goods' would stand on

carpet. By adding a good quantity of yellow to the blue, I devised an aqua tone to harmonize the concept in the flooring on that side; for the carpet on the other side, I specified a lightish violet. This contained an added factor: since violet is next on the electromagnetic spectrum to ultraviolet, it has built in associations with the future, time and space, which is always good in support of modern technology. The flooring in the central aisle, dividing the two sections, was to be light ash.

I do hope your head is not beginning to ache as you try to picture this colour scheme – it is important to remember that they were light, bright, but not at all strong Spring colours, and the essential harmony enabled us to use a more interesting colour scheme than would have been possible without this understanding. It would not have worked if any of the tones had not belonged to the Group I family. In fact, at one point, one of the graphic designers accidentally used the wrong orange – an autumnal tone – and everybody instantly reacted to the negative effect.

For the particular tone of light, clear violet in the carpet, the manufacturers took us over to their factory in Denmark for a day to work with their chief designer on the CADCAM (Computer-Aided Design, Computer-Aided Manufacture) system to ensure that we got it right. That was a wonderful experience for me.

Finally the cash desk was done in Spring green – clear and fairly strong. This provided the essential element of reassurance as people approach the till, and calmed fears that perhaps they should not really be making this

THE GREEN ON THE LONDIS SHOP WINDOW BALANCES THE RED AND ORANGE, REDUCING THE RISK OF CUSTOMERS FINDING THESE HIGHLY VISIBLE COLOURS INTIMIDATING.

purchase – could they really afford it? Did they really like it? Did it represent good value for money?

The day I presented my colour scheme to Comet, I did not meet the designers; I simply presented my ideas and visual aids, with exact colour specifications drawn from colours available in the marketplace, and then went away to await the decision. Two days later the company telephoned me and advised that they had decided to go with my scheme, and were going to commission me to work on the project with their designers. They told me who the designers were, and that they had instructed them to work with me and implement the colours as I advised.

I confess, I went a little pale at this. The design house in question was one of the biggest and most eminent in London, and they did not know me at all. I arrived for my first meeting with them filled with trepidation. These were not people who were accustomed to being told what to do with colour, and I had no way of knowing, although I felt I could guess, how they had responded to being instructed to do as they were told by some unknown female who had just appeared, as if from nowhere. I arrived at their offices and was ushered into a room where five people were assembled around the table. After the introductions, I sat down.

'We just want to know one thing,' the chief designer said. 'How did you persuade Comet to accept that colour scheme? You may not be aware of this, but our presentation last week was our second one; yours are exactly the kind of colours we had tried to persuade the client to consider with our first presentation. We know they are absolutely spot on. Why couldn't we convince them?'

I explained that I was working to a specific system, which enabled me to provide a written rationale in support of recommendations, and I asked to see their first presentation boards. As they were being sought out and brought, I said that I was prepared to bet that, whilst the bulk of the colours were probably in the Spring family, they had included some tones from another season, which had the effect of obscuring the clarity of the message, and also negated the Group I tones, making them appear cheap. It is a natural mistake, when one perceives a danger of something looking cheap, to introduce an element of something more classy or expensive-looking into the mix. In practice this only serves to exaggerate the cheapness. When the designers' first presentation board arrived, I was able to identify three Group II (Summer) tones in it. These presented a conflict which, whilst the Comet directors could not analyse a reason for it, simply turned them off.

From that moment, the designers and I worked happily together, and have been doing so ever since on many other projects. When the new megastore opened, it was clear that we had solved the eternal problem of store-opening events by converting sightseers into purchasers. The takings broke all previous records. For a couple of years after that, whenever I was introduced to anyone new at that design consultancy, I became accustomed to their saying, 'You must be the lady who did Comet in purple and orange!', though I eventually tired of explaining that it was not just any old purple and orange, but two very specifically harmonized tones.

LONDIS

The third example of effective use of the Spring palette involved the Londis Group. Londis is a co-operative of more than 1700 convenience stores throughout Britain. Their corporate colours were red and orange, and they had a chequerboard device on the fascia of all their stores. It was rather harsh and presented a mixture of tones, as the red was Group IV Winter and the orange was Group III Autumn. It was also not a well-balanced colour scheme. Londis was an extremely successful company nevertheless.

The Londis offer is all about convenience and personalized, friendly service. They knew they could not compete with the major supermarkets on price, as the latter always benefited from economies of scale and also did not have to pay staff overtime to remain open all hours. Their competitors were other convenience stores. Because of this price issue, the Spring environment was as appropriate to Londis as it had been to Comet, although for a different reason, in that it created a perception of a fair deal and value for money. The colours I recommended, however, were completely different.

The first question to be addressed was that of the entrance. Convenience stores are open late at night, and customers need more encouragement to come in; they need to be reassured. I recommended that red, with its potential for aggression and fear, be removed from doorways and the door surrounds, and I knocked back the red and orange on the decal (the permanent colours on a shop window) and introduced some green to balance it. I also warmed up all the white to a cream tone. Inside, I recommended more tones to communicate the nature of each sector – blue for frozen goods, red for special offers etc. Again I introduced green check-outs to replace red.

In the written rationale, I explained to the company that, although red had the advantage of maximum visibility, it must be used carefully. I also suggested that Londis should ideally consider a much greater influence of green, and I pointed out that the chequerboard device was essentially a Group IV design, which was not appropriate to Londis. They were not ready then to dispense with the chequerboard, but they did implement all the other recommendations, and it was very successful. Like Vax, they kept the palettes I provided and continued to apply them. I note that the whole of the front of the most recently refurbished Londis shops is now predominantly green, with orange – and the chequerboard has gone.

Here is a final thought for you about retailing. When you hear the names Shell International, BP, Esso, etc., what business comes to mind? Oil? Certainly, but these days, these companies are the world's biggest retailers.

CONCLUSION

The Emperor's New Clothes

I look around at the strident discord of life, especially in Western civilization, as we approach the end of the twentieth century, and I seriously wonder if humanity has lost the plot. We seem to have got all our value systems upside down, and we rush headlong down the Nowhere Path, wondering why we are not happy. We gravitate towards already overcrowded areas of the planet and conspire to convince each other that as long as enough of us are following the latest fashion it must be good. Have we completely lost the power of individual discrimination? Like the loyal subjects of the deluded emperor in the traditional tale, whose advisors persuaded him to parade through the town stark naked, in the certain knowledge that they could convince the people that he was magnificently arrayed in new finery, we all shout and cheer our approval of the most nonsensical concepts – just because everybody else is admiring them. We hesitate to emulate the little boy in the story, who turned to his mother and said, in a piercing tone, 'But Mummy! That man isn't wearing any clothes!' because we don't want to appear unsophisticated, do we?

This book is not designed to tell you what colours to use, but to heighten your awareness of the power of colour and how it can fundamentally influence your life. I want to persuade you to think for yourself, and give proper thought to what colours are right for you in any given situation – your wardrobe, your home, your product's packaging, your office decor – regardless of what colours are right for your best friend, your mother, your competitors, your favourite movie star or the latest supermodel.

It is often assumed that colour is rather a frivolous matter, not at all important compared with the practical considerations of life – essentially an adornment. But colour is at the very heart of our existence and can, more than anything, alter our perception of the world, which is the factor that truly determines the course of our lives. In a fascinating book about sacred geometry, Robert Lawlor observes,

> In science today we are witnessing a general shift away from the assumption that the fundamental nature of matter can be considered from the point of view of substance (particles, quanta) to the concept that the fundamental nature of the material world is knowable only through its underlying patterns of wave forms.

And,

Plants, for example, can carry out the process of photosynthesis only because the carbon, hydrogen, nitrogen and magnesium of the chlorophyll molecule are arranged in a complex twelvefold symmetrical pattern, rather like a daisy. It seems that the same constituents in any other arrangement cannot transform the radiant energy of light into life substance.

So it seems to be a universal law that underlying patterns are vital to life and, no matter how effective the individual parts of anything may be, if they are put together wrongly, they will not work. There are no bad colours, only bad arrangements.

A lot of people find it 'too difficult' to assert their own preferences in the matter of colour. There is a strong element of defeatism in that attitude. In clothes shopping, for example, the common perception is that there are only a few colours available to us – the 'in' colours this season. In my experience, this is a myth. The shop windows and fashion magazines may all be full of the 'in' colours, but the reality on the streets is that people are dressed in a myriad of colours, and every garment in the shops is usually offered in a choice of colours. I used to produce a newsletter for my personal clients twice a year, for which I scoured all the fashion shops and department stores and wrote an analysis of the scene, naming specific manufacturers and retailers. I might, for example, say something like, 'Don't be fooled into thinking that blue-green colour featured this season by Jaeger is Summer – it is actually a soft Autumn tone. Sonia Rykiel is featuring a nice Summer green.'

The process of researching this newsletter was endlessly educational, and I was constantly amazed at the vast choice available, even in these days of multiple shops. I realized, for example, that the personality of the buyer in a department store, or the owner of a smaller shop, will be reflected in the range he or she buys. A striking example of that occurred for me once in Selfridges, in London, when I was strolling through the Designer Room. A suit almost jumped off the rail at me: it was a Caroline Charles design, in rich tan, with a Paisley print in autumnal greens. Perfect. The style was exactly right for me, too.

I immediately asked to try it on and bought it, regardless of the fact that I had not planned a purchase that day, and it was very expensive. However, I estimated that, in terms of cost per wearing (the only way to consider the price of any garment) it was not expensive at all. I looked around at the whole Caroline Charles display, and it was almost exclusively autumnal, with Shetland wool sweaters in Fair Isle, glorious colours, soft, warm-toned brushed cotton shirts and other elegant suits.

A week later I had a meeting with a director at Harrods, and I wore my new suit. On my way to his office, I passed through Harrods' Designer Room. The Caroline Charles display there bore no resemblance to that of

Selfridges, just down the road. Here the suits were all solid colours, and it was pure Group IV – Winter. Royal blue, black, vivid jade green were the stars of this display. There was not a single item common to both stores. Later on in my meeting, I asked the director if the Fashion Buyer in the Designer Room was a dramatic-looking person, with great presence, probably dark hair and compelling eyes?

'You must have met her!' came the reply.

I had not met her, I explained, but the influence at work in that department told me all about her. Equally I knew that the buyer at Selfridges was an Autumn-linked personality.

It is a good idea, therefore, to find shops which more often than not echo your own ideas about colour and style, and to stick to them for as long as the same buyer is employed there. The aspect of a garment that you consider first is pure habit. Most people look at the shape and fabric first, rather than the colour, but this is not necessarily a good way to shop anyway, regardless of the colour issue, as often the best cut clothes do not have what is known as 'hanger appeal'. I found it quite easy to adopt the habit of considering colours first. It was a joy to discover that I could go through any shop or fashion department in a matter of minutes, if I homed in only on my kind of colours. I quickly progressed to the stage where it was as if the others did not exist – a common phenomenon of human awareness. Before that, I used to waste hours going through all the rails, considering garments which would never do anything for me. Such a waste of both time and money. I had an added bonus, too, as I learned to withstand pushy salespeople. Now the prime consideration for me was to buy a supportive colour and the prospect of upsetting or offending the salesperson came a very poor second to that. I found my confidence grew – I knew what I was doing.

Fashion retailers did not respond to the concept of colour analysis when it spread throughout the world in the early 1980s. They have the idea that it will limit people in what they might be persuaded to buy. One can see their point, but I would be interested to see what would happen if one of them were to try an experiment and present clothes already accurately ranged in the four seasons.

People often imagine that I am going to complicate matters. There are so many other considerations to get right – adding colour to the list is seen as the last straw. But in practice, if you get the colour right first, all the rest falls into place. The chief designer on the Comet project, described in Chapter Nineteen, told me that, whether he used this system of tonal grouping or not, since his experience with my work he always uses colour as the starting point for any project. He gathers the team together and instructs them to go away and consider the implications of the project, the values to be expressed, and come up with five key colours. A few days later, they all reconvene and thrash out the basic palette of five colours by a process of consensus. He said he could not believe what a difference this has made to his working life. Everything thereafter falls into place more naturally and more easily.

We all have aspects of our lives which we find unsatisfactory, but we can only address them when we are ready. We all know people who are overweight, who complain the whole time about being fat and about the negative attitudes of society towards fat people, but they never seriously get down to the job of losing weight. Others complain about their work and their boss, but they do not resign. We see the frustrated and unhappy ill-treated wife who never considers taking drastic action to improve her lot, either by standing up for herself or by starting divorce proceedings. We do not have the confidence to make major changes.

But suddenly one day, something strikes a chord, just at the right moment, and a resolution forms. Only then will we be really effective. Then it becomes easy. Our awareness shifts and old attitudes fall away.

It is my hope that this book will do that for at least some of its readers. If it doesn't do it for you, don't worry, but don't discard it. Read it again next year. By then you may be ready to stop following the crowd and throw your black shoes away.

INDEX